1956

W9-AEE-677

MATTHEW ARNOLD

A STUDY IN CONFLICT

"I say, the critic must keep out of the region
of immediate practice."

BY E. K. BROWN

MATTHEW ARNOLD

A STUDY IN CONFLICT

THE UNIVERSITY OF CHICAGO PRESS

THE UNIVERSITY OF CHICAGO PRESS, CHICAGO 37
Cambridge University Press, London, N.W.1, England

TO

E. J. PRATT

PREFACE

IT WAS Matthew Arnold's express wish," says G. W. E. Russell, the editor of his letters, "that he might not be made the subject of a biography." A few months before he died, Arnold deplored the appearance of Edward Dowden's *Shelley;* he thought that it came between the reader of Shelley's poems and the "ideal Shelley." Arnold's wish has been respected for sixty years. Apart from the speculative image presented in Mr. Hugh Kingsmill's *Matthew Arnold*, the only full-length figure that comes between the reader of Arnold's works and the ideal Arnold is the correct, cheerful, domestic Victorian gentleman who appears in Russell's edition of the letters, an edition mangled by the family blue pencil. If the materials for a detailed and revealing biography of Arnold exist, the secret has been well kept.

For some time there has been a promise of an edition of Arnold's notebooks, which has been under preparation by Mr. Howard F. Lowry and Mr. Waldo H. Dunn. I have been permitted to consult the notebooks in the Rare Book Room of the Yale University Library by the courtesy of the keeper, Professor Chauncey B. Tinker. They disclose a host of important facts about what Arnold read but relatively little of his responses to his reading and almost nothing of the impulses that led to his own works. They disclose almost everything one might care to know about his finances, which were more flourishing than I had supposed. They offer a detailed although incomplete record of his official

engagements, much information about his countless jour-
neys, and some about his social life. But these notebooks
are not journals. At best they supply a rather full framework for Arnold's life; they do not mirror that life or his
consciousness of it. One may still hope that journals will
find their way into print.

My concern (like Professor Lionel Trilling's in his
Matthew Arnold, to which I am much indebted for its
discernment and scholarly fulness in almost everything
that relates to Arnold's thought) is with Arnold's mind. I
have not tried to write a biography either of the man or of
his mind. What I have tried to do is much more limited: to
illuminate Arnold's writings by tracing the history of a
lifelong conflict within his personality. In the absence of a
full biographical record I have depended, of necessity, on
his writings, his letters, and the impressions of his friends.
It is not the whole of Arnold's personality that I have tried
to render. There are perhaps too many books that concern
themselves with Arnold as a whole. It is appropriate to
present special aspects at some length and thus prepare
the way for a full account and estimate. In *Studies in the
Text of Matthew Arnold's Prose Works* (1935) I tried to illuminate his personality, thought, and art by a study of his
revisions. The conflict which forms the subject of the present study will take the reader somewhat nearer to the center of Arnold.

For many years my interest in Arnold has been en-
couraged by Professor Chauncey B. Tinker. He has allowed me to encroach upon his time and to solicit his criticism with a generosity that has never faltered. Not only
did he open to me the treasures of the Rare Book Room at
Yale; he also allowed me to consult his own magnificent

private collection of Arnold material; and by his kindness
I am able to quote from the precious *Yale Manuscript* or
Balliol College Note-Book, a source of the highest importance. He has also supplied the copy of the famous cari-
cature in *Vanity Fair* (1871) from which the Frontispiece
has been prepared. He crowned his services to my study of
Arnold by reading the manuscript of this book, to its great
advantage. Mr. Lowry has also read the manuscript, and I
appreciate his kindness the more that he was obliged to steal
time from his presidential duties to do so. My friend and
former teacher Professor Louis Cazamian has done me the
tedious service of reading the proofs; and to his penetrating analysis I owe more than I can readily express. To
Professor Richard McKeon and Professor R. S. Crane,
both of the University of Chicago, I am indebted for their
aid in securing a grant from the divisional research fund
which expedited the final stage of preparation. To those
students in my courses on Arnold who have raised significant questions over the years I am no less grateful.

I regret that I have not been able to see Sir E. K. Cham-
bers' book on Matthew Arnold in time to draw upon it:
Nothing it contains invalidates any of the positions taken
in this study.

ACKNOWLEDGMENTS

THE quotations from *Matthew Arnold: How To Know Him*, by Stuart P. Sherman (copyright 1917, 1944), are used by special permission of the Bobbs-Merrill Company; the quotations from *Selections from the Prose Writings of Matthew Arnold*, edited by Lewis E. Gates, by special permission of Henry Holt and Company; the quotations from *The Poetry of Matthew Arnold: A Commentary*, by C. B. Tinker and H. F. Lowry, and from *Letters of Matthew Arnold to Arthur Hugh Clough*, edited by H. F. Lowry, by special permission of the Oxford University Press; the quotations from *The Use of Poetry and the Use of Criticism*, by T. S. Eliot, and from *Poetry and the Criticism of Life*, by H. W. Garrod, by permission of the Harvard University Press; and the quotations from *Unpublished Letters of Matthew Arnold*, edited by Arnold Whitridge, by permission of the Yale University Press.

TABLE OF CONTENTS

Coleridge failed in that attempt, happily even for him, for it was a struggle against the increasing life of the mind itself. The real loss was, that this controversial interest betrayed him into a direction which was not for him the path of the highest intellectual success; a direction in which his artistic talent could never find the conditions of its perfection.—WALTER PATER

CHAPTER ONE

The Problem: Poses and Uncertainties

FROM the time of its first appearance there have been two continuing lines of objection to the poetry of Matthew Arnold: that it was strangely inconsistent with his poetics and that in style it was astonishingly uncertain.

The hiatus between the doctrine in Arnold's Preface to his collection of 1853 and some of the pieces in that volume was immediately remarked upon by reviewers. Among the guiding principles in the Preface was the subordination of parts to the whole, the preference for a mighty "total-impression" rather than for "brilliant" "single lines and passages." Careful construction assuring the true relation of the parts to the whole was in Arnold's view the hallmark of a true artist. William Caldwell Roscoe, writing in the *Prospective Review*, was the first in an unending series of critics to wish that Arnold had pondered his own critical prose and profited by it. "Few men," he said, "have ever more systematically disregarded their own preaching."[1]* As wholes Arnold's poems gave Roscoe no pleasure; but here and there, in the occasional single lines and passages of which the author was so contemptuous, Roscoe could find "scattered rays of enjoyment." Roscoe did not revise his opinion as one collection of Arnold's verse followed another; four years later in 1858 he made it his principal objection to Arnold

* See Notes at end of book, pp. 187–217.

as a poet that he had "every where shown that he is deficient in the higher power of conception which requires unity."[2] A poem from an earlier collection reprinted in that of 1853 specially invited and received criticism on this score. Roscoe pointed to the close of "Tristram and Iseult," the tale of Vivien's seduction of Merlin. The material so strangely added here—that it was no part of Arnold's original conception of the poem we now know—Roscoe found to be "totally new and disconnected" from what went before.[3] The reviewer for *Fraser's Magazine* set the tone for a somewhat more friendly estimate of the poem: on the one hand, he said in more downright fashion than Roscoe that the tale of Merlin and Vivien "has absolutely no business where it is"; on the other, that in itself—as a single passage—it is "beautiful, exceedingly beautiful."[4] How natural the bewilderment of the early reviewers in the face of the Merlin-Vivien tale had been, the persisting uncertainty as to its place in the poem makes all too plain. Arthur Hugh Clough, for all his intimacy with the mind of the author, could make nothing of it. "The mist of more than poetic dubiousness closes over and around us . . . . and . . . . it is really all but impossible to ascertain" the real meanings of the tale. "Why or wherefore or with what purport, who will venture exactly to say?"[5] Mr. Tinker and Mr. Lowry are scarcely more definite: they suggest various meanings the tale may have—perhaps it may have more than one meaning—but they cannot pronounce with confidence.[6] The reviewer for *Blackwood's* attacked the structure of the poem more generally and pointed, like Roscoe, to the Preface. "Tristram and Iseult" is, he says, "terribly disjointed . . . . affording no trace of that symmetry of design, the lack of which in modern poetry Mr. Arnold has very justly deplored."[7]

The early reviewers made the same objection to the expansive similes which break the severe evolution of "Sohrab and Rustum" and "Balder Dead" and yet admitted that many of them were as single passages delightful;[8] they made it also to the close of "Sohrab and Rustum," the picture of the Oxus on its inevitable course to the Aral Sea;[9] they made it to the garland of pictures in "The Strayed Reveller."[10]

Wherever one looks for temperate criticism of Arnold as a poet, the objections of the early reviewers are reaffirmed. Richard Holt Hutton, a man of Arnold's generation, a devoted reader of his verse, and often its apologist, wrote the best general account of it to appear in the 1870's.[11] He has the same reservations about "Tristram and Iseult" as the early reviewers. It lacks "definite form and organisation"; it does not qualify for the name of "narrative"; but in occasional passages, in paintings of objects or of moods, it is often "lucid" and "exquisite." In the same decade Henry Buxton Forman repeats the reproaches of the early reviewers against the straggling similes in "Sohrab and Rustum" and "Balder Dead."[12] Before these similes Professor H. W. Garrod, who has been in our time the wisest defender that Arnold's poetry could find, can do nothing but ring the changes on the "beautiful, exceedingly beautiful" of the early reviewers and concede that the brilliant passages do not melt into the general pattern of the whole. "Gentler spirits (among whom I would wish to be)," he says, "may be forgiven if they tire less easily of beautiful images and are not disposed to fret too much over what element they may contain of the irrelevant and adventitious." His tone is the same when he speaks of the close of "Sohrab and Rustum," "that passage . . . . which if the poet had been either Homer or Sophocles, if he had wished to obey any rules there may be either for tragic or for epic art, would not have been there at all."[13] A violation of Arnold's classical principles, the passage may be, but Mr. Garrod will say for it that it is the greatest part of the poem. Mr. Carleton Stanley, a more recent defender, complains in the old manner that in "The Strayed Reveller" nothing is firmly grasped.[14]

The old objections are reaffirmed; and new objections of the same kind are raised to poems in which the early reviewers had detected no fault of structure. Stuart Sherman, who appears almost to have modeled his intellectual and spiritual life on Arnold's, says of "The Scholar Gipsy" and "Thyrsis": "Now, to speak it frankly the thought in these much-praised elegies is a bit too thin to bear triumphantly the weight of all the flowers which Arnold has strung upon it. He presents in them both an appearance, an unwonted appearance, of dallying by the wayside, of digressing, of indulging in a moral holiday."[15] To the last two stanzas of "The Scholar Gipsy" a dozen critics have paid homage as beautiful, exceedingly beautiful in themselves only to call in question their place in the pattern of the poem.[16] That they have some place in it I have sought to show elsewhere;[17] but that Arnold has elaborated and complicated them far beyond what their function requires or will bear is, I think, indubitable.

The examples of dissatisfaction that I have given I could easily multiply without going outside the range of genuinely perceptive criticism. But there is no need to add to the number. It is clear that there has been a continuing line of objection to Arnold's poetry as defective in structure. Arnold objected eloquently to the critics who "will permit a Poet to select any action he pleases, and to suffer that action to go as it will, provided he gratifies them with occasional bursts of fine writing, and with a shower of isolated thoughts and images."[18] It was because of the taste he scourged that his own poetry was enjoyed. The problem raised by the gaping inconsistency between the poet's precepts and his performances is what now interests me. Disturbing as it would be in any poet that what he wished to achieve and what he did achieve were wholly unlike, how much more disturbing is it when the poet was a born critic of literature, above all of poetry, and at the very least the greatest critic of his age!

II

The same problem in slightly different guise is presented by the extraordinary unevenness, the uncertainty of Arnold's poetic style. Everyone knows that he lacks a distinctive manner of his own, differing in this from Tennyson and Browning, Swinburne and Rossetti, Hardy and Housman. But by unevenness of manner and uncertainty of style I mean much more. I mean by uncertainty of style the multitude of passages such as these on which the early reviewers pounced:

> Still gazing on the ever full
> Eternal mundane spectacle.[19]

or

> No, I nothing can perceive
> Without that, all's dark for men.[20]

or such lines as later critics have marveled at:

> Who prop, thou ask'st, in these bad days, my mind? . . . .[21]

the opening of a sonnet which closes with some of the most melodious and memorable lines of the century; or

> There the pines slope, the cloud-strips

which offended the ear of Lionel Johnson;[22] or, if I may quote an old abomination of my own:

> Not by their hands who vex the patient ground,
> Mov'd only; but by genius, in the strife
> Of all its chafing torrents after thaw,
> Urg'd.[23]

By unevenness of manner I mean the apparently unconscious juxtaposition of the admirable and charming in image, language, construction, or rhythm with the impossible. When Hermod in "Balder Dead" is on his way to Hela's realm, the underworld, he approaches a golden bridge kept by a damsel, the queen's servant. Arnold has described Hermod's journey in terms which make it appear grand and terrifying; for nine days and nights he has ridden unresting and alone, in silence, along the edge of roaring streams and through cavernous valleys. At length he reaches a narrow golden bridge only to find his passage barred:

> But as when cowherds in October drive
> Their kine across a snowy mountain pass
> To winter pasture on the southern side
> And on the ridge a wagon chokes the way,
> Wedg'd in the snow; then painfully the hinds
> With goad and shouting urge their cattle past,
> Plunging through deep untrodden banks of snow
> To right and left, and warm steam fills the air,—
> So on the bridge that Damsel block'd the way.

Mr. Garrod observes that the simile is not without grotesque suggestions. To be downright, it is wholly inappropriate. What went before was beautiful, what comes after is no less; but the lapse is complete.[24]

How grave a problem such an unevenness presents, Saintsbury suggests in his criticism of "The Church of Brou," one of the most illuminating pages ever written on Arnold's poetry:

> If as no critic ever can, the critic could thoroughly discover the secret of the inequality of *The Church of Brou*, he might, like the famous pedant, "put away" Mr. Arnold "fully conjugated in his desk." The poem . . . . is divided into three parts. The first, in trochaic ballad-metre, telling the story, is one of the poet's weakest things. You may oft see as good in Helen Maria Williams and the Della Cruscans. The second, describing the church where the duke and duchess sleep, in an eight line stanza of good fashion, is satisfactory but nothing more. And then the third, after a manner hardly paralleled save in Crashaw's *Flaming Heart*, breaks from twaddle and respectable verse into a rocket-rush of heroic couplets, scattering star-showers of poetry all over and round the bewildered reader.[25]

That "The Church of Brou" is as horribly uneven as Saintsbury says, I do not think there can be any doubt. All that one misses from his judgment is the curious history of the poem. It first appeared in the collection of 1853; was reprinted in 1854 and 1857, with no significant change; was preserved in the first collected edition, of 1869; because of the severe and unanswerable criticisms directed at the inaccuracies in the telling of the legend and in the description of the settings, the first two parts were removed from the edition of 1877, where the beautiful third part stood by itself; the parts were brought together again in the edition of 1881, and the poem has come down in this form, which is essentially its first as well.[26] To the extraordinary unevenness the master critic who wrote it appears to have remained quite insensitive his whole life long.

It is the more remarkable since Arnold was quite extraordinarily sensitive to unevenness in the poetry of others. The principal reason he gives for compiling anthologies from Wordsworth and Byron was his conviction that their excellent pieces suffered from being shouldered by inferior pieces in the collected editions.[27] Just two years or so before restoring to his own collected edition the inferior parts of "The Church of Brou" he wrote of Wordsworth: "In his seven volumes the pieces of high merit are mingled with a mass of pieces very inferior to them; so inferior to them that it seems wonderful how the same poet should have produced both. . . . . Work altogether inferior, work quite uninspired, flat and dull, is produced by him with evident unconsciousness of its defects, and he presents it to us with the same faith and seriousness as his best work."[28] His remarks on Byron are even more interesting. It was Arnold's view that Wordsworth wrote excellent poems and tiresome inferior pieces, without recognizing the difference, and that Byron wrote poems in which the excellent and the inferior mingled. He accepts Swinburne's judgment that "Byron rarely wrote anything either worthless or faultless." The total impression left by Byron's longer works is unsatisfactory, dim, and indistinct; but "bursts of sentiment" and "bursts of incident" of very high excellence will "occur in the midst of poems which must be admitted to be but weakly conceived and loosely combined wholes."[29] The "bursts" are "vivid, powerful and effective." Even in short poems Arnold can admirably mark an unevenness of texture. He quotes the "four immortal lines from Burns" which Byron chose as epigraph for *The Bride of Abydos:*

[8]

> Had we never loved sae kindly,
> Had we never loved sae blindly,
> Never met, or never parted,
> We had ne'er been broken-hearted.

They have, he says, a deeper poetic power than anything that Byron wrote; but "a whole poem of that quality Burns cannot write; the rest, in the *Farewell to Nancy*, is verbiage."[30]

Of the unevenness in his poetic manner, of the uncertainty of his poetic style, we must say as we said of the failure of so many of his poems as wholes, that in the work of so admirable a poet-critic it is in the highest degree disturbing. The most eminent and the most fastidious of his successors in the Oxford chair of poetry, Andrew Cecil Bradley, says that "Arnold's taste in language" is "so delicate and true" that, if he were to discover himself dissenting from it, he would at once assume himself to have been mistaken.[31] One critic could not say more for another. Yet himself Arnold could not save. The critic, whose taste has such a perfection of delicacy and truth, turning poet will write:

> One morn, as through Hyde Park we walk'd,
> My friend and I, by chance we talk'd
> Of Lessing's famed Laocoön.[32]

On the appalling flatness of these lines, flatter surely than any of the lines Arnold singles out to represent Wordsworth at his flattest, we have the comment of the poet-critic who in our time occupies a function somewhat like that of Arnold in his. Mr. Eliot observes: "It may be said of Arnold's inferior work as was said of that of an inferior poet, that he faggotted his verses as they fell, And if they rhymed and rattled, all was well. Of course, we do not judge Arnold as a poet by such effusions as this, but we cannot be blamed for forming a lower opinion of his capacity for self-criticism. He need not have printed them."[33]

Why was the critic so incapable of self-criticism? Why could he not see the texture of his poetry as it really was—often rough and without pattern, more often thin? Before an answer is attempted, we should inquire whether questions of the same sort may be raised concerning Arnold's manner and method in prose.

III

In his need to invest his substance with a form ideally appropriate to it, Arnold devised for himself a prose style which is among the most remarkable in English. It has never received the full analysis or the detailed estimate for which it so obviously calls. The most perceptive treatment of this, as of so many aspects of Arnold's art and thought, is in the introduction Lewis Gates wrote for his volume of selections from Arnold's prose.[34] Gates discriminates four kinds of style in his author: the severe exact style of his educational reports and the books which arose from them, the least personal of his styles; the familiar easy style of most of the literary essays and the blander parts of his social criticism; the no less familiar but much harsher style in which he conducts controversy on any topic that arouses the evangelist in him; and the emotional, highly wrought style of a few essays and a number of passages, used when Arnold is paying heartfelt tribute to someone who, like George Sand, had helped to form his youth or to some ideal to which his spirit vibrates, such as Oxford's devotion to beauty. Much the greater part of Arnold's prose, as Gates rightly says, belongs to the second or the third kinds of style. This is not the place for a full study of Arnold as a stylist in prose: that is the matter for a book. Still, on Gates's classification, there are two comments which are inescapably necessary.

The emotional and highly wrought style appears in his prose much more often than Gates's account suggests, not, it is true, in wholes but in parts. At the crucial moment in many an essay it replaces the second or the third style. The essay on Byron is written in the second style; but as Arnold approaches the climax in his enthusiastic account of the personality of Byron—a personality which Arnold, following Goethe, sets above all other poetic personalities —the style rises:

> He threw himself upon poetry as his organ; and in poetry his topics were not Queen Mab and the Witch of Atlas and the Sensitive Plant— they were the upholders of the old order, George the Third and Lord Castlereagh and the Duke of Wellington and Southey, and they were the canters and tramplers of the great world, and they were his enemies and himself.

And in the following paragraph once more, and in a manner yet higher and more poetic:

> But when this theatrical and easily criticised personage betook himself to poetry and when he had fairly warmed to his work, then he became another man; then the theatrical personage passed away; then a higher power took possession of him and filled him; then at last came forth into light that true and puissant personality, with its direct strokes, its ever-welling force, its satire, its energy, and its agony.[35]

The powerful rhythms, the delicate balance, the repetitions, the sense for climax—they are all appeals not to reason but to feeling. Arnold is not now submitting a reasoned case to the reader's intelligence; unconsciously, perhaps, he is laying siege to his emotions. There are passages of a similar tone in almost all the first series of *Essays in Criticism* (they do not come in the first and second essays of the series, which are strictly argumentative, as the nature of their subjects requires), in the lectures on Homer and on Celtic literature, and, I think, in all the later literary essays except for the essay on Shelley—an arraignment rather than an estimate—those on late discoveries such as Tolstoi and Amiel, and that on English prose style, the so-called "introduction" to the edition of Johnson's selected *Lives of the Poets*.[36]

This observation is the first to which Gates's account leads; and it is necessary to make it because the use of such prose as this in critical writing is in opposition to Arnold's theory of the function of literary criticism. He is rigorous in his reproof of Macaulay for his ill-judged use of rhetoric in literary criticism. The paper "A French Critic on Milton" was written four years before the essay on Byron; and in the estimate of Macaulay with which it opens the strongest stress is upon his substitution of rhetoric for criticism, his appeal to the emotions of the reader rather than to his intelligence. "A reader," he says, "who only wants rhetoric, a reader who wants a panegyric on Milton, a panegyric on the Puritans will find what he wants. A reader who wants criticism will be disappointed." Macaulay, he says, is deceptive, "wrapping in a robe of rhetoric the thing [he] represents."[37] Arnold's rhetoric is very different from Macaulay's. Arnold could not have written such a salute to Milton as this, which he quotes for reproof: "There are a few characters which have stood the closest scrutiny and the severest tests, which have been tried in the furnace and have proved pure, which have been declared sterling by the general consent of mankind, and which are visibly stamped with the image and superscription of the Most High. Of these was Milton."[38] Yet Arnold's account of the subjects of Byron's poetry in contrast with the subjects of Shelley's is just as truly rhetorical as this salute to Milton. As much as Macaulay, he is engaged in wrapping his matter in a deceptive robe of rhetoric. Shelley was not uninterested in "the canters and tramplers of the great world," he was not silent concerning the misdeeds of the champions of the old order, some of the very champions whom Arnold mentions by name. Has Byron himself outdone the line: "An old blind, mad, despised and dying king"?[39] The significant difference between Arnold and Macaulay is that Macaulay has a constant manner, and this is rhetorical, but Arnold resorts to rhetoric only now and then. Just as in his poetry he has no assured manner of his own by which we can mark him, so in prose he is various and multiform.

The second observation which Gates's account requires is of a more fundamental kind and more obviously concerns the theme of the present study. Gates says:

It is undeniable that when apart from his *Letters* Arnold's prose as a whole is compared with that of such a writer, for example, as Cardinal Newman, there is in Arnold's style, as the ear listens for the quality of the bell metal, not quite the same beautifully clear and sincere resonance. There seems to be now and then some unhappy warring of elements, some ill-adjustment of overtones, a trace of some flaw in mixing or casting. Are not these defects in Arnold's style due to his somewhat self-conscious attempt to fascinate a recalcitrant public? Is it not the assumption of a manner that jars on us often in Arnold's less happy moments?[40]

This is admirably expressed, and there can be no doubt that Gates is pointing to a true defect in Arnold's style in prose. Mr. Garrod is thinking of the same defect when he speaks of Arnold's manner as "stagy."[41]

[13]

When a writer's style lacks the fulness of sincerity, when it makes one think a manner has been put on, and that manner a stagy one, when it suggests an unhappy warring of elements, the probable conclusion is that in the writer's self there is internecine conflict, that he is in the process of remaking the self. Perhaps one should also conclude that he is trying to screen from his own view as well as from the suspicion of others some elements in the self which are strong and demanding. These conclusions will be strengthened if it can be shown that the author's touch was uncertain, that he did not always know, or even generally know, what was the appropriate tone to maintain, that he was in the habit of having second thoughts about the tone of a work or a passage.

IV

That Arnold's touch in prose was uncertain his critics have always believed. It is perhaps enough to look at what three of them have said, one at the outset of Arnold's career as a writer of critical prose, another shortly after his death when his reputation as a prose-writer stood very high, and the third in our own time. The first considerable study of Arnold as poet and critic appeared in the *British Quarterly Review* for October, 1865, soon after the publication of the first series of the *Essays in Criticism*. The article is friendly, even cordial, and the subject was much pleased by it. Arnold's uncertainty of touch is firmly marked:

> But what if the advocate of an authoritative Academy to suppress all that is provincial, Asiatic, Corinthian, can himself be convicted of the very departure from urbanity which he deplores? It may be done. If not Corinthian, is it not at least provincial to describe the *Church and State Review* and the *Record* as the "High Church rhinoceros and the Evangelical hyaena"? Mr. Arnold's preface to the *Essays* [the *Essays in*

Criticism are intended] is full of life, full of humour; but it is occasionally Corinthian. Thus when deprecating certain phrases which connected his criticisms on translators of Homer with his position at Oxford, he says: "My native modesty is such that I have always been shy of assuming the honourable style of Professor, because this is a title I share with so many distinguished men—Professor Pepper, Professor Anderson, Professor Frickel, and others —who adorn it, I feel, much more than I do." This is thoroughly provincial; what follows is worse.

"I serve under an illustrious Chancellor, who translates Homer, and calls his Professor's leaning towards hexameters a pestilent heresy. Nevertheless, that cannot keep me from admiring the performance of my severe chief; I admire its freshness, its manliness, its simplicity, although, perhaps, if one looks for the charm of Homer, for his play of a divine light. . . . . *Professor Pepper must go on, I cannot.*"

The flash of painful humour is wilfully Corinthian.[42]

What befell the passages singled out as examples of the irruption into Arnold's prose of the qualities he had condemned in others it is interesting to note. In 1869 in the second edition of the *Essays in Criticism* the "flash of painful humour" concerning the Homeric exploits of the earl of Derby is gone. The rest remains. Yet the reference to the three absurd pseudo-professors is of a piece with the reference to the earl of Derby.

As an example of criticism at the height of Arnold's reputation for prose, I take the judgment of another Oxford professor of poetry, delivered from the chair. In his lectures on *Life in Poetry, Law in Taste*, given between 1895 and 1900, W. J. Courthope remarks:

I know of no more salutary corrective for the vanity of the criticism which trusts solely to the infallibility of its own intuitions, than a comparison of the principles recommended by Matthew Arnold with his practical application of them. For example: "To reach through Culture the firm intelligible law of things." Think then of Matthew Arnold's application of this principle to English society, and "the law of things" which was disclosed to his perception; his division of his own nation into Barbarians, Philistines, and Populace—could any phrases and

[15]

terms be found to-day more esoteric, more unmeaning, more obsolete? Or again: "An increased desire for sweetness and light." Was it sweetness and light that suggested to Matthew Arnold's imagination the simile of the three Lord Shaftesburys? Or: "All the bent which we call Hellenising." Hellenising, nevertheless, was of no avail to prevent that fine and beautiful taste which once embodied itself in *The Scholar Gipsy* and *Thyrsis* from conceiving and committing to print the following sentence: "From such a spectacle as that of poor Mrs. Lincoln—a spectacle to vulgarise a whole nation—aristocracies undoubtedly preserve us!" A form of Culture which is constantly violating the first principles of good breeding will scarcely enable us to renew the decadent life of Poetry.[43]

Again it is interesting to note what befell, what had befallen long before Courthope wrote, the passages to which he objects. In *Literature and Dogma*, looking for a clear and vivid means of bringing home to his readers the narrow anthropomorphism of conventional Christian conceptions of the Divine Personality, Arnold had likened the Trinity, as currently conceived, to a triad of three variants on the contemporary philanthropist, the seventh Earl of Shaftesbury. The Father was "a sort of infinitely magnified and improved Lord Shaftesbury, with a race of vile offenders to deal with, whom his natural goodness would incline him to let off, only his sense of justice will not allow it"; the Son was "a younger Lord Shaftesbury, on the scale of his father and very dear to him, who might live in grandeur and splendour if he liked, but who prefers to leave his home, to go and live among the race of offenders, and to be put to an ignominious death, on condition that his merits shall be counted against their demerits, and that his father's goodness shall be restrained no longer from taking effect, but any offender shall be admitted to the benefit of it on simply pleading the satisfaction made by the son"; and the Holy Spirit was "a third Lord Shaftesbury, still on the same high scale, who keeps very much in the background, and works in a very occult manner, but very efficaciously nevertheless, and who is busy in applying everywhere the benefits of the son's satisfaction and the father's goodness."[44] Of the aptness and vividness of the simile there can be no question. That no use of his name could have been more appalling to the devout and rigid earl, Arnold does not seem even to have considered. In the Preface to the popular edition of the book Arnold remarks: "The sole notion of *Literature and Dogma*, with many people, is that it is a book containing an abominable illustration, and attacking Christianity." He speaks of Shaftesbury as one who has earned the deference of "all who can appreciate one of the purest careers and noblest characters of our time" and announces that having learned that his illustration "has given pain" to Shaftesbury, he will "expunge" it.[45] That an experienced man of letters and one who had made himself intimately familiar with the religious attitudes of his contemporaries should have supposed that his simile could fail to give pain is what astonishes. The allusion to Mrs. Lincoln comes in *Culture and Anarchy*;[46] it was in the text of the periodical essays and in that of the first edition in book form; from the second it was excised. Why, there is no way of knowing for sure, but once again one may suppose that Arnold had not at first weighed the measure of offensiveness in his observation with an artist's accuracy.

For the criticism of our time Mr. Garrod may speak. He has so friendly a manner in voicing his objection that it seems to be dissipated as soon as it is uttered; but the phenomenon he is noting is the same as Gates detected:

There is a good deal of the poseur in him—I not only concede it cheerfully, but, to be honest, I enjoy it. I like the good art of it, and the supercilious airy amiability with which it is managed. If Matthew Arnold carried into political and social criticism the manner of a man of letters, he also carried into the criticism of literature—or liked to think that he did—the air of a man of the world. The rôle afforded him artistic delight; and on the whole it was well suited to him. The part of it which he carries least well is the cosmopolitan pose, the affectation of being born on the continent. But in general his bland finish of manner, and the delicacy of his irony are beyond praise. If he is not the greatest of English critics, his make-up of being so is in itself a piece of greatness; and not to enjoy it is a piece of stupidity.[47]

The uncertainty of touch, the attempt at a pose, at seeming what he is not, point to some inner conflict, central and enduring. The man who is at one with himself, as Walter Pater says in "Diaphanéité," makes of his "expressions," whether these be acts or words or thoughts, "a kind of determinate expression in dexterous outline of one's personality."[48] Sainte-Beuve habitually accomplishes this, and so, to take a lesser example, does Lowell. It is the man who is not at one with himself whose personality is expressed by a wavering outline, retouched as his dominant mood varies and blurred where he is unwilling to disclose something which is there but which he wishes to reshape. What the essential inner conflict in Matthew Arnold was I shall now attempt to indicate.

V

On the twenty-ninth of October, 1864, from the Oxford chair of poetry, Matthew Arnold delivered a discourse on "The Functions of Criticism at the Present Time."[49] In the opinion of his interpreters this discourse is among Arnold's main achievements. For Stuart Sherman it is "an important essay"; for W. C. Brownell "a stimulating essay";

[18]

for Lionel Trilling a "great essay"; for Herbert Paul "perhaps the best [essay] he ever wrote"; and Saintsbury explains the reason why so much interest and so much praise attach themselves to the discourse when he says that it is "the general manifesto . . . . of its author's literary creed."[50] It has recently given the theme to a penetrating lecture by Professor Geoffrey Tillotson.[51] It is not going too far to claim that Arnold's literary criticism is read by most of those who care to know it well in the light that the principles asserted in this essay provide. Its place as the opening piece in the first series of *Essays in Criticism* shows that it was intended to serve somewhat in this way.[52]

The key word in it is "disinterested." Arnold opens the most important section of the paper by saying: "It is of the last importance that English criticism should clearly discern what rule for its course, in order to avail itself of the field now opening to it, and to produce fruit for the future, it ought to take. The rule may be summed up in one word—*disinterestedness*."[53] The complexity of "disinterestedness" has been emphasized by Mr. Tillotson, who analyzes the content of the term and decides that "what was scarcely satisfactory was the grouping of all this wriggling life under the abstract heading of *disinterestedness*."[54] My analysis will differ from his but move in the same direction. The idea denoted by this key word is not by any means so simple as first appears. In one meaning of the word Arnold is recommending not a critical faculty or disposition but rather a critical strategy, a quality in one's mode of presenting one's ideas which is essential if these ideas are to become widely operative. For a Victorian critic's ideas to have their full chance of being weighed by his compatriots for their intrinsic worth—and it is to be noted that Arnold here specifically recommends disinterestedness simply to his contemporaries in criticism and not to critics in general—for the Victorian critic's ideas to affect opinion and civilization as they deserve to do, the critic will need to write in a disinterested manner. The examples that Arnold offers make plain that he is laying an emphasis on strategy, on the production of an effect. Cobbett, he says, had lost all chance of a quiet hearing because in the eyes of his compatriots he stood "blackened . . . . with the smoke of a lifelong conflict in the field of political practice"; and Carlyle, his by his "furious raid into this field with his *Latter-day Pamphlets*"; and Ruskin very recently, his by his "pugnacious political economy."[55] Their compatriots, clinging to the established thing, are suspicious of advocates of direct and specified change, of critics who can be ticketed as having programs which they burn to put into practical effect. National opinion in Victorian England— and Arnold has his eye on the Victorian middle class to whom the future belongs—is pliable only when it is worked upon in a roundabout fashion, by ideas which have the innocent appearance of generality.

Disinterestedness has, however, another and a profounder meaning in the discourse. It denotes a critical faculty or disposition as well as a critical strategy. To become the opposite of disinterested is mortal not to the critic's effectiveness upon the opinion of his time alone but to his excellence. Here Arnold would seem to be addressing all critics. "The rush and roar of practical life," he says, "will always have a dizzying and attracting effect upon the most collected spectator, and tend to draw him into its vortex"; and once whirled about in that vortex, interested in the success of some practical program and in the defeat of its rivals, committed, let us say, to the success of some organized party in church or state, he will become incapable of seeing things as they really are. "In this way the pursuit of truth becomes really a social practical pleasurable affair, almost requiring a chairman, a secretary, and advertisements, with the excitement of an occasional scandal, with a little resistance to give the happy sense of difficulty overcome; but, in general, plenty of bustle and very little thought."[56] Criticism written in the interest of party will be criticism warped and partial; it will not be and cannot be criticism deriving from a vision of things as they really are. And no criticism which does not derive from this can be valid.

In this essay Arnold does not stress a difference between the disposition and the strategy. It is marked in all its force in a novel which appeared a few years after the *Essays in Criticism*, Thomas Hardy's *A Pair of Blue Eyes*.

The tragic situation at the close is of the kind in which Hardy's imagination always took the strongest delight. Harry Knight, a radical intellectual, and Stephen Smith, his protégé, have each loved but once, and both have loved Elfride Swancourt. Stephen's love was at first warmly returned, to the point that Elfride eloped with him, intending to marry him; later, under the spell of Knight, she rejected Stephen. Most of her charm for Knight lay in her appearance of perfect innocence; and when he heard of her earlier attachment, presented to him in a vicious light, he broke with her. He did not know that Stephen was the man she had loved. Just before the novel ends, with her funeral, Stephen and Knight, meeting by chance in London, enlighten each other. Neither knows that she has just died. As Knight learns how really innocent the relation between Elfride and her former lover had been, he adopts an "air of renunciation and apparent indifference"; and "as his interest increased" he "persevered in the tone and manner of a disinterested outsider." Stephen, for his part, gathering ever greater assurance that all love between Elfride and Knight was dead and that the future belonged to him, tried for the same tone "with all the strategy love suggested." The innermost being of each man was vitally concerned in the outcome of the conversation; nothing could ever matter so much as this to either; but in the choice of words, in the assumption of tone and manner, each behaved as if he were considering some quite imaginary situation, each employing with a subtle art the strategy of the disinterested outsider. The conversation is in the sharpest contrast with another held between them on the following day when they surprise each other in the Wessex train which is taking them to Elfride's home. Now the disguise of a disinterested strategy is no longer possible, and the naked intensity of a desperate interestedness runs through all they say.[57]

In the development of Arnold's personality there are times when he is truly disinterested in disposition as these two lovers never were; there are times when he is as eager to win his readers to a moral or intellectual opinion as the lovers were to win Elfride and, as in their first conversation, proceeds in the belief that an air of total disinterestedness will be a powerful instrument toward the accomplishment of his aim; there are times when he considers it useless, as they did in their conversation in the train, to keep even the air of disinterestedness; and there are times when he is impelled irresistibly by the old Adam in him to speak with the naked intensity of interestedness. To examine him as he passes through these various phases of thought and feeling is to come very close to the center of his being and to observe his art as well as his personality from a new point of view.

CHAPTER TWO

Poetry and Theory of Poetry

IT IS natural to begin with the deeper of the two forms
of disinterestedness, with the disposition, the disinterested frame of mind, conceived as a necessity if one
would possess one's own spirit in serenity and if one would
see things, literary and other, as they really are. The attraction such an ideal had for Matthew Arnold declared
itself early. In his Rugby prize poem of 1840, on Alaric,
the opportunity to celebrate heroic action is refused. "Of
the thrilling and picturesque incidents in Alaric's career,
death and burial the boy made no use. Material which the
imagination of a Scott or even a Macaulay might have
made vivid and absorbing is left undeveloped and unil-
lumined."[1] What dominates the poem and makes its mood
is the poet's pleasure in stillness and reverie. The pictures
which are most highly wrought are those of Rome quietly
awaiting the barbarian incursion and quietly enduring the
barbarian rule. Alaric, in possession of the city, does not
rage or exult; he silently and meditatively surveys it and
his own past. The Oxford prize poem on Cromwell, composed three years afterward, is no less significant. The
ideal of serenity, of the possession of one's own spirit, enters into conflict with the ideal of heroic and responsible
action which was dictated by the subject itself. Cromwell
comes before us reluctantly abandoning

> Some shadowy vision of a tranquil life,
> Of joys unclouded, years unstirr'd by strife.[2]

[24]

Such quiet, in which his personal nature would have found its account, was forbidden him because the necessities of the time prescribed action. Arnold's references to the value of a serene and meditative life are much more than incidental—the contrast between life of this sort and the life of action is essential to the structure of the poem. The following year, in 1844, he composed his sonnet on Shakespeare, and what he pours into it is his admiration of serenity. The detachment of Shakespeare,

Self-school'd, self-scann'd, self-honour'd, self-secure,[3]

from all care for his fame, present or to come, is the stamp of his peculiar genius. He possessed his own spirit, wrought it out in the forms which furnished it with supreme expression, and in this he found fulfilment. In a jotting of a slightly later time Arnold returns to the theme of Shakespeare's serenity, finding in it the elusive essence of the man and saying of the moralist, an inferior type, that Shakespeare extorts his admiration because the moralist is "conscious of his own imperfection and strain."[4]

In the first collection of Arnold's poems, *The Strayed Reveller* (1849), the contrast between the way of action and strain and the way of detachment and serenity is presented in many forms. The sonnet with which it opens and which serves as a clue to the intellectual and spiritual purport of the book establishes a contrast between the beautiful silence with which the phenomena of nature perform their functions and the noise and turmoil characteristic of human schemes and actions.[5] Stillness as a beauty of nature recurs in four other poems in the small collection —"Mycerinus," "Resignation," "To a Gipsy Child," and "The Voice."[6] In the great silence the sounds of human

[25]

origin are trivial and frivolous. Stillness as an essential quality in the ideal of human character is explicitly set in contrast with its opposite in the two highly philosophic lyrics "The World and the Quietist" and "In utrumque paratus."[7] Stillness and the detachment which it favors are the theme of most of the yearnings in the most frankly personal of all the poems in the volume, the long piece with which it closes, "Resignation," in which the poet communes with his sister and confidante "K." Here, for the first time the innermost concerns of Arnold are disclosed. The detachment is not a hermit's, it is not exclusive; it is that of the man who has no personal end which absorbs him, no ambition or passion which directs his course and puts blinkers upon his eyes. The disinterested man remains clear of vision and able imaginatively to enter into the manifold experiences of other men and even of natural objects. His impersonality is not a loss of contact with the stream of life but rather a qualification for feeling and understanding its currents. By virtue of his "quiet" and of a "rapt security," the disinterested man can "draw homewards to the general Life," a spiritual aim which Arnold sets for all good and wise men.[8] Elsewhere in the collection human excellences closely linked with detachment, such qualities as serenity and steadiness of spirit, appear again and again.[9] It is easy to develop from this book the type of character to whom the young poet is drawn: simple and unified like the duke of Wellington,[10] serene like Shakespeare, living in others and in his creations like the poet in "Resignation"[11] and the young artist in "The Strayed Reveller."[12] It is given its strongest statement in the tribute to Sophocles:

> But be his
> My special thanks, whose even-balanc'd soul,
> From first youth tested up to extreme old age,
> Business could not make dull, nor Passion wild;
> Who saw life steadily, and saw it whole;
> The mellow glory of the Attic stage,
> Singer of sweet Colonus and its child.[13]

In another poem, not published until 1852 but composed in the same year in which *The Strayed Reveller* was published, "Stanzas in Memory of the Author of *Obermann*," Arnold is concerned with the immense difficulties which beset a man of the nineteenth century who would attain the ideal qualities of character. The main portrait is flanked by those of Wordsworth and Goethe, Wordsworth a symbol of tranquil and serene humanity nourished by the silence of nature, Goethe a symbol of the spirit bred in clearness of vision and steadiness of will and therefore capable of coping with the stridencies and confusions of a later time without being invaded by them. To one born so much later and living so much in the society of his time as Arnold, the ways of Wordsworth and Goethe are not viable:

> What shelter to grow ripe is ours?
> What leisure to grow wise?[14]

Solitude is necessary if a modern man would cultivate the virtues of detachment; one cannot as in earlier times participate largely in the process of social activity and yet possess one's own spirit. The pace is now too dizzying, the activity too complex. The ideal of the disinterested character is reasserted:

> He who hath watch'd, not shar'd the strife,
> Knows how the day hath gone;
> He only lives with the world's life
> Who hath renounc'd his own.[15]

This is the advice that Senancour tenders. Everything that has preceded it suggests that for Arnold it will be valid and that he will accept it. He does not. He says he will leave half his life behind him as he turns from Senancour but that he will turn, will enter the "world." No argument to justify the turning is offered; there is no suggestion that Senancour's rigor is mistaken or that the world has either less danger to the spirit or more worth for it than Senancour has allowed. All that Arnold says is that he firmly trusts he may remain unsullied by the world, in it but not of it; and if he can so remain, he knows he will not be disowned by spirits such as Senancour even if they disapprove his decision. The poem is unsatisfactory because it is not a completely articulate communication: there is something that Arnold is withholding from us—the motive for turning toward the world, for running those perils to the disinterested frame of mind which he has drawn for us with such force and conviction. Even in 1849 there is an inner debate between the impulses toward detachment and the impulses toward action—for to be in the world is to be active; and twenty years will pass before the debate reaches its climax and moves toward a resolution.

To the young Arnold's devotion to detachment—it is worth noting that in "The Function of Criticism" he speaks of the power of disinterestedness as "the Indian virtue of detachment"[16]—his early letters bear as full witness as his poems. Most of his dissatisfaction with Clough stemmed from his distaste for the Faustian elements in that restless spirit. As early as 1848 he is trying to convert Clough to the Indian virtue of detachment as put forward in the Bhagavad-Gita and in doing so offers his earliest explicit description of the psychological disposition which he will later call "disinterestedness": "The Indians distinguish between meditation or absorption—and knowledge: and between abandoning practice, and abandoning the fruits of action and all respect thereto. This last is a supreme step and dilated on throughout the poem."[17] What Arnold is presently seeking to attain is not the supreme step but the preference for meditation over knowledge and the abandoning of practice for the habit of observation. The attainment of either of the lesser steps would increase his simplicity, his possession of his own spirit. When the earliest of his letters to Clough are read in the light of those belonging to the winter and spring of 1853—replies to protests from Clough that Arnold had been withdrawing from him and to lamentations that their intimacy had been unfortunate for both—it becomes clear that practically from the outset of their correspondence Arnold had implied and suggested objections to the elements of intellectual instability and moral feverishness in his friend.[18] It is no less clear that simplicity, steadiness, and stillness were qualities that Arnold admired and sought rather than securely possessed. They were to be attained only at the cost of a severe intellectual and spiritual regimen. Arnold would have Clough believe that he had never sought to withdraw from him as a particular individual; what he will admit is that at about the time when he was putting together his first collection he had experienced "a strong disposition to intellectual seclusion, and to the barring out all influences that I felt troubled without advancing me."[19] The same sense that his intellectual and moral state was insecure appears in a letter to his sister and confidante where he concedes that he and his poems alike are but "fragments" as a result of his "weakness."[20]

Aware of his weakness to an even painful degree—of his "want of intellectual robustness" as he calls it in another letter—[21] he discerned two paths which might conduct him to strength. One was the path of action—the world. In Lord Lansdowne's circle, to which he had come in 1847, a career of political action inevitably presented itself to his imagination; and his letters during the four years he remained with Lansdowne abound in excited allusions to the immediate political issues of the time. He rejected a political career because he did not believe that it was ideally suited to his inner nature; as he says in a letter to his reformer brother, William, written after he had begun his work as an inspector of schools, it would not be action according to his own personal way, and "I cannot bring myself to do more than a halting sort of half-work in other people's way."[22] The opposition between a path of action and the alternative path is clearly defined in a letter to Clough in which he suggests that "a great career is hardly possible any longer—can hardly now be purchased even by the sacrifice of repose, dignity and inward clearness."[23]

Repose, dignity, and inward clearness—it was to these shining virtues of the disinterested frame of mind that he would direct his steps, abandoning practice and preferring meditation, along a path which led away from action. In what did this path consist? First of all, in books, the reading and the writing of them and the reading as yet more than the writing. The main motive for his resort to literature appears as early as 1851 when he tells his sister that he is reading grave and ancient writers and withdrawing "more and more from the modern world and modern literature, which is all only what has been before and what will be again, and not bracing or edifying in the least."[24] Even in political journalism the note akin to dignity, repose, and inward clearness was what stirred him. In the midst of the French upheaval in 1848 Carlyle wrote an article for the *Examiner;* to Clough, Arnold describes this as "deeply *restful* . . . . amidst the heat and vain words";[25] and to his mother, after repeating the phrase "deeply restful,"[26] he went on to define more explicitly the source of the strong attraction, finding it in Carlyle's power to lay aside loud and superficial facts in favor of the "ideal invisible" root of the matter. In a word, the aid he drew from Carlyle's article was toward contemplating the revolutions of 1848 without febrile excitement, toward being a disinterested and understanding onlooker, seeing things as they really were:

> He who hath watch'd, not shar'd the strife,
> Knows how the day hath gone.[27]

In his praise of the ancients in the Preface to his collection of 1853 Arnold likewise reflects his own search for dignity, repose, and inward clearness. Those who have frequented ancient authors and are at home in ancient civilization bear, he says, the marks of "a very weighty and impressive experience"; and this has brought to them a "steadying and composing effect upon their judgement" and not only on their judgment on letters but no less on their judgment of men and events. It is such a "discipline" as this that he has sought though, as he confesses, he may still be far from having attained it. In firmly marking *Empedocles on Etna* as a poem stemming from the Greek decadence he pauses to suggest the ethical and intellectual qualities of Greece at the moment of her perfection: these are "the calm, the cheerfulness, the disinterested objectivity" which are the object of his own long quest.[28]

The value of "disinterested objectivity" was for the young Arnold an intrinsic value: it was to be sought, and he sought it, not primarily for anything that it might enable a man to do, either as a poet or as a citizen, but for what it enabled a man to be. A disinterested man was the kind of man that he desired to be, whether his life took him into the world or not.

II

What of the strategy of disinterestedness? This, too, has a history going back to the early poetry and early thinking about poetry. It is also related to the curious attitude he assumed toward his friends. One of his intimates at Balliol was John Duke Coleridge, the son of Sir John Taylor Coleridge, a lifelong friend of Dr. Thomas Arnold's. In 1844 Coleridge became engaged to the sister of John Billingsley Seymour, another Balliol man of Arnold's academic generation, whose untimely death the year before had been a college tragedy. In notifying Arnold of the engagement, which had so many claims upon his interest, Coleridge appears to have taken some credit to himself for telling such tender news to one whose chilling appearance of indifference to his friends' concerns was a matter of common reproach. The indifference, Coleridge thought, was perhaps no more than a deceptive appearance. The reproach, Arnold replies, "is an old subject"; and the supposed indifference is not genuine. "I laugh too much," Arnold continues; and when he would be serious, his friends suppose that he is laughing up his sleeve. A vicious circle is created; and he must seem to laugh when he would not. Even after such an explanation, which would appear to clear the air very thoroughly, Arnold goes on in an embarrassed and woefully self-conscious manner:

It is impossible for me to say more about your marriage than that I congratulate you, which I do very sincerely. I know you are shaking your head. You told it me, you know, as briefly as you could, and as late as you could, and it is a delicate subject at best. . . . . It was a great surprise. I had heard you speculate, too in so disengaged a way, but a few months before on the desirableness of marriage. *Mais nous avons changé tout cela*. I see I shall be incurring fresh suspicions, so I shall quit the subject. I could speak of it more freely than I could write.[29]

The coolness of manner, the relapse into the comic, are the marks of one who would keep his distance even from his intimates and have them do the same with him. The comic element in Arnold's manner was at this time exceedingly strong, and perhaps it never left him. Another Balliol friend, J. M. Hawker, writes of him in 1843 as uttering "as many absurdities as ever, with as grave a face" and in another letter of the same year, relating his journey with Arnold into Devonshire, mentions how "Matt . . . . pleasantly induced a belief into the passengers of the coach that I was a poor mad gentleman, and that he was my keeper."[30] The earliest letters to Clough are heavily marked by comic exaggerations. The examination of conscience concerning his adequacy for his duties as a temporary teacher at Rugby in the letter of March, 1845, is among the most comic things that Arnold ever wrote.[31] It was doubtless because of the comic manner and the coolness of his attitude that, when his poems appeared, his sister Mary was deeply surprised by the seriousness and intensity which run through so many of them, the "something which such a man as Clough has, which I did not expect to find in Matt." The poems, she thought, were "almost like a new Introduction to him." They could have come only from some one who had stood "face to face with life and asked it, in real earnest, what it means."[32] Of Arnold's being such a person his manner was a deliberate denial. It was the outcome of a strategy, and the purpose of that strategy would appear to have been to encourage detachment, to correspond with that "utter want of preju- dice"[33] in which, as he once said to Coleridge, he gloried.

In the letters to Clough, despite the tentative and even confused fashion in which Arnold there deals with aesthet- ic principles, one can trace his devotion to the disinter- ested strategy and his extreme dissatisfaction with its op- posite, so strongly characteristic of Clough's verse. How acute the dissatisfaction—amounting surely to nothing short of repulsion—must have been we may discover from a letter written in December, 1847, in which Arnold frankly says in returning a set of Clough's poems: "I have had so much reluctance to read these . . . . that I surely must be destined to receive some good from them."[34] Nor is his apology for such "a beastly vile note"[35] a few days later convincing as to anything more than shame at an ex- hibition of gross manners. What it was that repelled him appears in the same letter: "Rare as individuality is, you have to be on your guard against it—you particularly." Shortly afterward he drew a distinction between the po- etry of the Victorian time and earlier poetry in terms which are full of awareness of how difficult it had become to employ the strategy of disinterestedness. In earlier times, even as late as the seventeenth century, a poet was fortunate in having a "*smaller harvest than now*," a slighter weight of ideas; and he was therefore free to devote him- self to the elaboration of a form most perfectly appropriate to express what ideas he had. In Arnold's time, burdened almost inevitably with such a multitude of ideas, the poet was all too likely to throw these at his audience unclothed in the splendors and felicities of an adequate structure and idiom.[36] Poetry of such imperfect form could be but a personal communion between poet and reader: it would have adopted the strategy of a pure lyric. More fully in the profound letter of February, 1849, Arnold outlines the ideas which separate his poetics from the poetics implicit in Clough's verse (and as every reader of Arnold knows, implicit, too, in so much of what he himself was to write). The peculiarity of poetry, he says, is form; wealth and depth of matter are "superfluous" in the poet as such. There are two aspects to form: expression and conception, otherwise expressed, style and structure. When the style and the structure are both in perfect keeping with the matter, the greatest poetry issues. To see deeply into one's matter is not to see poetically. Arnold quotes a line from his own "Resignation": "Not deep the Poet sees but wide."[37] The wide vision which he attributed to Homer in a sonnet belonging to the collection of 1849[38] is an instance of disinterestedness in the deeper sense of a disposition. The organization of a poem so that the vision it expresses shall be wide rather than deep is an instance of disinterestedness as a strategy.

"The Strayed Reveller," in its succession of decorative pictures and in the tenuous suggestions of character and idea which they carry, is an illustration of what the strategy of disinterestedness can achieve. Arnold concludes with the judgment that Clough does his best work in the hymn, "where man, his deepest personal feelings being in play, finds poetical expression as *man* only, not as artist:—

but consider whether you attain the *beautiful* and whether your product gives PLEASURE, not excites curiosity and reflexion."[39] In the hymn as Arnold conceives it here, the strategy is the reverse of disinterested: the communion is intimate and in intention complete and of the most direct kind. Arnold was all his life to be a severe judge of the hymn and very nearly insensitive to any poetic worth a hymn might have. The *Golden Treasury*, as he was to say in the Celtic lectures, "is a monument of a nation's strength"; the *Book of Praise* "is a monument of a nation's weakness."[40] To say that Clough was at his best in the hymn was to say that his poetry was at the exact opposite from the kind of poetry that Arnold at this time, and indeed in general, most admired and most sought to accomplish.

From his early gropings toward a theory of poetry it is not a difficult turn toward his practice in the collection of 1849. The title poem, "The Strayed Reveller," has already been named; it is in every respect the sort of poem the author of the observations to Clough might be expected to write. It is almost insignificant in substance, unless a series of delicate moods may be regarded as substance. Its power is eminently a power of structure and style. The group of exquisite pictures, more vivid, as Professor Douglas Bush remarks, than Arnold could later match, conveyed in language of extraordinary limpidity and finish, resembles some old idyll. To come back to the phrases in which Arnold had pointed out what he thought amiss in Clough's verse and turn them now toward a positive sense, he is here expressing himself not as a man but as an artist; he is intent upon attaining the beautiful; he is, above all, intent upon giving pleasure. Nor, despite the link with Marguerite[41] and the sadder among the emotions which his experiences with her inspired, need "The Forsaken Merman" be spoken of in very different terms. The personal emotion has been so transmuted by the strategy employed that the effect is one of aesthetic pleasure, contrived, as one sees on beginning to analyze the structure, by triumphant artistry. Not all the poems in the collection are of this kind. Already, Arnold occasionally exhibits that penchant for moralizing self-analytic poetry which he was deploring in Clough. "A Modern Sappho" and "Resignation" are such poetry. But as yet the instances are few. Poetry of this kind, as the later collections of his verse would show, it was natural for him to write; it was to escape encouraging whatever within himself would lead to the writing of such poetry that he was so eager to seclude himself from the intellectual and spiritual influences of his time and from so many of its type experiences. Only by doing this could he so arrange his inward life as to attain the disposition of disinterestedness and rest securely in it; only so could he allow to the strategy of disinterestedness its fullest scope.

The next state in his use of that strategy was in his adoption of myth in preference to more subjective poetic forms. By 1852 he had become aware that for him belief in the primacy of pure form, the belief that matter was superfluous in poetry, was not a doctrine by which he could adequately express his poetic powers: it required the suppression of too much within him. In October of that year he states to Clough the position he was to take in the Preface of the following year: the subject is everything, and form, whether of structure or of style, is but its garment. Nevertheless, in abandoning his conviction that by concentration

on form the poet may and should give a wideness and generality to his thoughts and feelings and thus escape interestedness, he was by no means abandoning, he was not
even qualifying, his devotion to the strategy of disinterestedness.[42] How true this is we may see by the character
of the poems which illustrate the new theory. In "Sohrab
and Rustum," Arnold is communicating through a myth
something of the quality of such a complex father-son relationship as he had had; in "Tristram and Iseult," something of the complex triangular relationship in which for a
time he had stood with Marguerite and another woman,
probably Frances Lucy Wightman; in "Balder Dead,"
something of the pathos of a poet cast upon an iron age.[43]
The mythic element comes to veil personal emotions even
in poems which are in part lyrical, such as "The Scholar
Gipsy" and the "Stanzas from the Grande Chartreuse."
Arnold's own feelings are there; but they are not there un-
disguised. How often, too, and beginning with the first of
the Obermann poems has Arnold chosen to express his
deepest feelings, his innermost thoughts, in poems where
the main theme is a friend or an honored artist whose
death he mourns. Strong personal feeling is in the elegies,
but it is projected toward another being or else generalized
as a grief for mankind or for man as he was at that particular period in his history:

> Wandering between two worlds, one dead,
> The other powerless to be born

or, as the idea was expressed in a more homely fashion by
another Victorian Oxford scholar, with jam yesterday and
jam tomorrow, but never any jam today. In the elegies
there are also moments in which the strategy of the pure

lyric is employed, is forced upon the poet by the painful intensity of his self-preoccupation. At such moments he writes as he did in "A Modern Sappho" and "Resignation." But intense and memorable as such passages are, they are but moments. The strategy of disinterestedness is at work in the narratives, in the mythic lyrics, and in the elegies, not always with the same force and fulness, to be sure, but in a degree which significantly affects the impact that a poem has upon the reader.

III

It is time to return to the deeper form of disinterestedness, the disposition whose attraction underlay so much of Arnold's earlier poetry, and inquire how it fared in the course of the 1850's. In the collection of 1849 thought played but a small part. Most of the poems in that collection square with a reflection of Arnold's in that curiously assembled "note-book" which Mr. Tinker and Mr. Lowry call the *Yale Manuscript* and which through Mr. Tinker's kindness I have been able to consult. Arnold there remarks: "To feel simply the simple feelings of humanity voila the natural life of man: to prolong, fix and dwell upon these by harmoniously expressing them, voila the natural life of the poet, and art—what can be done more than to arrange in the best way so as to produce the fullest most undisturbed effect—to recount a fact of interest with the most perfect limpidity."

The attitude persists in "Memorial Verses," the lament for Wordsworth written in the spring of 1850. The dead poet is set beside Byron and Goethe, and his gift is praised as superior to that of either contemporary. Byron is drawn as the poet of passion, Goethe as the poet of thought,

Wordsworth as the poet of joy in the aspect and influence of natural objects. The opposition between Goethe and Wordsworth—the heart of the poem—is suggested in terms of a passage in the *Georgics*, Arnold closing his tribute to Goethe with these lines of reservation:

> And he was happy, if to know
> Causes of things, and far below
> His feet to see the lurid flow
> Of terror and insane distress,
> And headlong fate, be happiness.[44]

He is recalling the great passage (ii. 490–97) in which so many have believed[45] that Vergil was describing the principal poet of thought in his time, Lucretius, the lines beginning

> Felix qui potuit rerum cognoscere causas

and which may be rendered as: "Happy is he who has learned to know the causes of things, who has put in subjection beneath his feet all terror and inexorable fate, and the outcry of the greedy grave." Beside the poet of thought, Vergil set a poet of another kind, his own:

> Fortunatus et ille deos qui novit agrestis
> Panaque Silvanum senem Nymphasque sorores

"And happy also is he who has known the gods of the countryside, Pan and old Silvanus and the sister nymphs." Of these lines there are no verbal reminiscences in the "Memorial Verses"; but, stripped of their myths, these lines say what Arnold says in his final tribute to Wordsworth:

> Keep fresh the grass upon his grave,
> O Rotha! with thy living wave!
> Sing him thy best! for few or none
> Hears thy voice right, now he is gone.[46]

What precedes these lines is a paean to Wordsworth's gift for "fixing the natural life of man" and for rendering this "with the most perfect limpidity." In contrast with such a gift as this, Goethe's power of thought is dismissed as but a minor accomplishment.

By 1852 Arnold was coming to believe that thought must play a primary role in the work of a modern poet who should be adequate to the function of poetry in his time. "Modern poetry," he writes to Clough in the autumn of that year, "can only subsist by its *contents*: by becoming a complete magister vitae as the poetry of the ancients did: by including as theirs did, religion with poetry, instead of existing as poetry only and leaving religious wants to be supplied by the Christian religion, as a power existing independent of the poetical power."[47] It was no longer enough to devise beautiful dreams and to play with delicate moods and thus encourage a feeling of distance and poise in one's reader, to the end that he become disinterested in feeling. The essential responsibility of the modern poet was now to think. For the author of "The Strayed Reveller" the accomplishment of this newly perceived duty could not be easy, for he continued to believe that poetry should be beautiful and that, as he said in the Preface to the collection of 1853, it should be possible "to derive enjoyment" from it.[48] The poetry of thought, undertaken by a modern weighed down by the multitude of ideas with which he must come to terms, was all too likely to come short in beauty and in the provision for enjoyment. What was even graver, it was likely by excess of emphasis on one level of existence, the intellectual level, to violate the ideal of disinterestedness.

Arnold's first great effort to satisfy his new conception

was *Empedocles on Etna*, which may be described as a prolonged struggle with thought. The first phase in the intellectual life of Empedocles was a manifestation of the disinterested disposition in intellectual terms. In Arnold's plan for the poem he spoke of this phase as one in which Empedocles "sees things as they are—the world as it is—God as he is: in their stern simplicity."[49] In the poem itself he represents Empedocles in Wordsworthian verses, looking back with nostalgia toward this irrecoverable time when he and Parmenides could think without becoming all intellect and nothing else and

> . . . . receiv'd the shock of mighty thoughts
> On simple minds with a pure natural joy.[50]

So long as thought was but one of their activities, so long as they retained "balance," the outcome of their thought was a mood of serenity, of happiness, of "purest peace." In his final phase Empedocles sadly addresses himself:

> A living man no more, Empedocles!
> Nothing but a devouring flame of thought—
> But a naked eternally restless mind,[51]

ever at variance with his fellows in intellectual discourse, incapable of entering into their natures, separated also from the panorama of natural objects and incapable of achieving oneness with nature, cut off from the nonintellectual parts of himself, fragmentary, distorted, dispirited, incurable. Arnold is presenting a terrifying contrast between a state in which the intellect plays its appropriate part in the total activity of a distinguished human being and a state in which it has run wild and consumed everything else. In the first state the person has steadiness and wholeness of vision, he is like the Sophocles of the 1849 sonnet; in the second, everything he looks upon is a blur of meaningless and valueless gray.[52] "The subtle contriving head" had been fatal to the vision and serenity which mark the disinterested disposition. Men such as Empedocles has become in his final phase are "thought's slaves,"[53] just as truly and disastrously as Tristram became passion's slave or as Clough became the slave of a scrupulosity in religious feeling. In the speeches of Empedocles, as John Campbell Shairp remarked to Clough,[54] Arnold was writing out some of his own thoughts, and these thoughts were those in which he was nearest to Clough; indeed, some of the stanzas have an impressive likeness to the more philosophic passages in Clough's early lyrics.[55] It was natural that what displeased Arnold in Clough displeased him also in his version of the late Empedocles. The position to which Empedocles had come was wholly incompatible with the disposition of disinterestedness.

That disposition is, however, reflected, although with no accompaniment of deep thought, nothing which could raise the poem into a true *magister vitae*, in the songs of the harp-player Callicles, and notably in the last of these, with which the poem ends. Arnold suppressed *Empedocles on Etna* for fifteen years and allowed it to creep back into print in the *New Poems* of 1867, only under the patronage of Browning, "a man of genius whom it had the honour and the good fortune to interest."[56] The harp-player's songs were to have a very different fate: they were restored to print in 1855.[57] The difference in fate is of the highest significance, for these songs are not unlike the classical pieces in the collection of 1849; they are brilliant successes in Arnold's earlier manner, where the rest of the poem was a venture in a new direction, so imperfectly successful as to displease its author. In trying to produce a poetry of thought, he had merely produced a poetry of the diseases of thought. It was said that the harp-player's songs were in Arnold's earlier manner; but it must be added that, without any loss in beauty or in the provision of enjoyment, they present a somewhat broader vision of life than the earlier classical pieces. The last song, a work of extraordinary beauty, does so most of all. The first half of it has to do with natural objects, the second with the supernatural; and there is no conflict, the supernatural beings move among the natural objects with a harmonious ease. Apollo and the Muses, representing thought as well as beauty, as they have done throughout the poem, offer an interpretation of the universe in which there is no fever or distortion:

> First hymn they the Father
> Of all things; and then,
> The rest of immortals,
> The action of men.
>
> The day in his hotness,
> The strife with the palm;
> The night in her silence,
> The stars in their calm.[58]

The quietness with which these lines move is a perfect medium for the "repose, dignity and inward clearness" of the mood and the meaning. The thought is not a disease but a single element in the balance of a perfect being. The serene and contemplative wisdom of the harp-player is a mark of the disinterested disposition; he thinks as he perceives and feels, without bias or heat, and he sees life steadily and sees it whole. "Not deep the poet sees but wide."

Empedocles on Etna is notable not so much for what it achieves as for what it attempts —Arnold's first effort to involve thought in a poem of length and complexity and yet to preserve the disinterested disposition. It points forward to other poems in which the attempt will be repeated. Most clearly it points toward "The Scholar Gipsy," which is intellectually the most impressive poem of the collection which appeared in the following year, 1853.

Like *Empedocles on Etna*, "The Scholar Gipsy" is a poem of discontent with intellectualism. Once more the poet is concerned with the diseases of thought rather than with its ideal or normal operations. In a famous stanza he places Goethe upon the "intellectual throne" of the nineteenth century.[59] Knowing the causes of things, as Arnold had said in the earlier "Memorial Verses," Goethe could read the diseases of the modern mind. His speech from the throne was wholly of ailments and anodynes. In the din of modern intellectual debate the head is overtaxed and the heart paralyzed; purposes wither and vision is obscured. The gipsy had fled from the less strident debates of a simpler Oxford, the Oxford of Laud. Not in the intellect but in intuition he placed his trust. As books are the instruments of the intellect, natural objects are for him the instruments of intuition; as logic is the exercise of the intellect, self-communion is for him the exercise of intuition; and as many persons resort to books and the exercise of logic and achieve no considerable intellectual outcome, so he may require to give a whole life to the meditation on natural objects and the practice of self-communion, with no valid intuition coming as reward. When he fades from our sight, the gipsy is still without a valid intuition; but he is still governing his life on the assumption that only so may such an intuition be attained; and unless it is attained, one has nothing fit for trust. The gipsy has had a precious incidental reward: he has become a disinterested being, in an eminent degree characterized by repose, dignity, and inward clearness, at one with himself and without the strain and imperfection of the moralist.[60]

The most successful of Arnold's attempts to deal poetically with the intellect in its normal operations and to find a place for it within the disposition of disinterestedness belongs to 1855. It is the "Stanzas from the Grande Chartreuse." The disinterestedness is essential to the structure of the poem. It opens with a survey of the monastery and its inmates, marked by the sort of discernment which implies sympathy. Arnold then imagines himself as reproached by men of the critical spirit who inquire whether he has abandoned their views and fallen a victim of the appeal of the religious faith from which the monastery has come. To the men of the critical spirit he rejoins:

> I come not here to be your foe!
> I seek these anchorites not in ruth,
> To curse and to deny your truth.

And of the monks, touched on with such sympathy, he nevertheless observes:

> Not as their friend or child I speak!

The picture of the monastery is balanced by a picture of the modern world. The poet speaks with almost breathless admiration of the progress in exploration and discovery, in transport and communications; he responds to the appeal of gaiety and movement. But for all his sympathy with the manifestations of the modern world, he underlines his own distance from them:

> We laud them, but they are not ours.[61]

Between the creed and way of life of the Carthusian and the creed and way of life of the busy modern, he places another creed and way of life, to which he subscribes. It derives from the melancholy of the essential Romantics, of Senancour and Byron and Shelley. But the very structure of the poem is proof that Arnold does not hold the creed and way of life as the Romantics did, for in his description of it he is almost as disinterested as in his description of the monk and the busy modern. He describes the Romantic position not as one in which he firmly stands but as one which is his merely because he belongs to the sad transitional age between the old order of Christian Europe and the new order of science and technology. Had he been born into the twelfth century, it is implied he would have been a monk; had his birth been delayed into, say, the twenty-second, he would be a man of science or industry. In intellectual terms the disinterested disposition could not be carried farther without reaching pure Pyrrhonism. Already it has come into conflict with essential qualities of the mood of disinterestedness. The dispirited relativism in which Arnold's intellectual attitude comes to rest in the "Stanzas from the Grande Chartreuse" is quite incompatible with the serenity, the true repose, of the disinterested man. The formidable truth which the "Stanzas" may have shown to Arnold, and clearly show to us, is that a disinterested fashion of presenting the ideas which recommended themselves most strongly to him as a modern man was not to be reconciled with the presentation of the ideal of human character he had formed, the man of dignity, repose, and inward clearness, serene and unharassed. I quote again from the *Yale Manuscript*. Arnold observes: "Man has limited faculties and very little from without is sufficient fully to employ them. Those are happiest in whom the equilibrium between the supply and the receptive power is best maintained."

There was no good solution for the problem. The modern poet must, he had decided, be a poet of ideas. The disposition of disinterestedness was not something to be narrowed to purely intellectual terms. The kind of ideas a modern poet must form—critical, relativist, tentative—were unthinkable in a character such as Sophocles or the duke of Wellington or the gipsy. Whether Arnold ever became clearly aware of the impasse to which he had come, there is no means of knowing. But the direction of his next major effort in poetry is suggestive. He wrote *Merope*.

Merope is primarily form. In his Preface he says that he wished to convey to those who have no Greek some impression of the "power of true beauty, of consummate form,"[62] in which classical poetry is unrivaled. His reason for turning to a poetry of form is given in a letter to his sister "K." He says:

> People do not understand what a temptation there is, if you cannot bear anything not *very good*, to transfer your operations to a region where form is everything. Perfection of a certain kind may there be attained or at least approached without knocking yourself to pieces, but to attain or approach perfection in the region of thought and feeling, and to unite this with perfection of form, demands not merely an effort and a labour, but an actual tearing of oneself to pieces, which one does not readily consent to (although one is sometimes forced to it) unless one can devote one's whole life to poetry.[63]

Arnold clearly is saying that the poetry of form is easier than the poetry in which form and thought are equally important and their union achieved; I believe his remarks also reflect a sense of his failure in the poetry of thought. I do not think a poet is likely to speak in such a defeated fashion unless he has experienced a crushing defeat, a defeat in his creative life. It is true that Arnold goes on to give worldly motives for his reluctance to tear himself apart: to imply his sense of responsibility to provide for a large family; to imply that tearings of one's self to pieces were scarcely compatible with the stolid routine of the Education Department, the only means that he had been able to find for the provision of his family. In saying and implying what he did, undoubtedly he was telling the truth; but I doubt that he told the whole truth or that it would have seemed so inescapably the truth to him if there had not been a failure in the deepest places of his art and character.

The appeal of the mood of disinterestedness accounts for the most original element in Arnold's handling of the story in *Merope*. The dramatic force in the story as it had come to him lay in a conflict between the essential goodness of Cresphontes, his wife Merope, and their son Aeptus, on the one side, and the essential evil of Polyphontes, on the other. The traditional Polyphontes is like Claudius in Hamlet but without the Danish ruler's amorousness. He slew Cresphontes, married (or wished to marry, in some versions) the widowed Merope, and planned to slay Aeptus. The Polyphontes of Arnold is very different: he is intended to be a man "for the ruin of whom, we may in spite of his crime feel a profound compassion."[64] He slew Cresphontes, but the state of the nation appeared to him to require it; he offered to marry Merope, but it was not from lust but rather from consideration of her queenly quality and a wish to do her honor; he had no design on the young Aeptus except to make him

[49]

his heir. We are to believe in his sincerity when he says at the opening of the play:

> But, Merope, the years advance;—I stand
> Upon the threshold of old age, alone,
> Always in arms, always in face of foes.
> The long repressive attitude of rule
> Leaves me austerer, sterner, than I would;
> Old age is more suspicious than the free
> And valiant heart of youth, or manhood's firm
> Unclouded reason; I would not decline
> Into a jealous tyrant scourged with fears,
> Closing, in blood and gloom, his sullen reign.
> The cares which might in me with time, I feel
> Beget a cruel temper, help me quell.[65]

He is asking for aid in his effort to retain a disposition "unclouded" by bias and free of ugly passions. He insists soon afterward that, although the slaying of Cresphontes was to his "interest" because it brought him to the throne, it was not an interested action but one prompted by conscience and therefore disinterested. He reflects in a manner very reminiscent of his creator:

> Most men are led by interest; and the few
> Who are not, expiate the general sin.[66]

Late in the play Merope pays tribute to his consideration for her, his wish to make amends, his unselfish devotion to the welfare of the state:

> So much is due to truth, even tow'rds our foe.[67]

And over his corpse Merope makes a funeral speech in which she weighs his one deed of violence and the personal ambition which may have been among his motives against his many moral and political virtues and confesses that she does not know, after twenty years, whether he was a good man or a bad. Coming upon Polyphontes' own professions of virtue, Merope's uncertainty prevents us from feeling that the slaying of Polyphontes was an act of ideal justice. Arnold is inviting the reader to refrain from taking sides in the drama, inviting him to survey the scene and conclude that each character acted for the best as he conceived the best. It is as if we were given an Iago who believed fully in his own virtue and had high reasons of state for inflaming Othello with suspicions of his wife or as if we were asked to believe that in César Grandet's avarice there was perhaps nothing more reprehensible than an aversion from riotous living and a laudable desire to provide for his wife and daughter. If Shakespeare or Balzac had insisted on making such points as these, the reader would not participate in the action, feel with the characters, as now he does. To see an action or a character from a multitude of points of view, each presented as neither more nor less valid than the rest, is a discipline in serenity, but it is fatal to that intensity of emotion which great tragedy must stimulate.

The end of *Merope* is disconcerting. Readers have long found it so, beginning with members of Arnold's family. The poet's admissions are significant. "It is true," he writes to one, "that Polyphontes is the most interesting personage, I think, though I suppose Merope ought to be." To another he writes: "The most attractive [personage] I certainly agree with you is Polyphontes."[68] To present the antagonist as equal in interest and attractiveness with the protagonist is to express the disinterested disposition in all its fulness; to present the antagonist with traits even more interesting and attractive is to allow the disinterested disposition to overreach itself. In either arrangement the tragedy cannot stir the degree of pity and terror we expect from tragic art. The quest of disinterestedness has here precluded the achievement of a great poem.

Nine years were to pass before *Merope* was to be followed by another volume of verse. Among the many reasons which are offered for Arnold's turning from verse to prose the inconsistency of the ideal of the disinterested disposition with success in the kinds of poetry which he believed a modern poet should attempt may be not the least cogent.

CHAPTER THREE

The Formation of the Critic

DURING 1856, in the months before he turned to the composition of *Merope*, Arnold went back to a subject which had long fascinated him, the character and intellectual system of Lucretius.[1] The drama in which Lucretius was to have been the principal personage "was, apparently, intended to have been Arnold's *chef d'œuvre* in poetry." As early as 1849 he bade himself in his notebook "Chew Lucretius"; and as late as 1886, when he had arranged to retire from the Education Department, he wrote of his Roman play as a work he had hoped to execute his whole life long and would even yet attempt if the "inward monitor" did not warn him that the time for it had passed.[2] The climax in his long preoccupation came in 1856 when he planned his reading to encourage composition and did, indeed, write a little, at least, of the play. In 1858, with *Merope* out of the way, he returned to the project, but with what result it is impossible to say. What befell Arnold's ideas about Lucretius and his world is a type of what befell many of the ideas he had considered expressing in verse. They became the theme of a passage of prose criticism.

In his inaugural lecture from the chair of poetry, "On the Modern Element in Literature,"[3] delivered in the autumn of 1857, the most strongly felt passage is one which deals with the virtues and defects of Lucretius and the great period in which he lived. The virtues of the man and the age are seen to be great. The age was quite simply the greatest in the history of the world. The age of Pericles, with which it was natural for Arnold to compare it, was of infinitely smaller range and on an immeasurably slighter scale both in material events and in the qualities of human relationships. Lucretius was both "a great poet" and "a great philosopher." He and his age were eminently modern in the special sense Arnold gives to the word—highly civilized, complex, and eternally interesting. But along with the other leading poets of the age Lucretius is deficient. Horace was a worldling. He was an example of poise, but his poise was acquired not by bringing into balance the deepest interests of man but rather by leaving most of them out of his conception of a valid ideal. Vergil, "the most beautiful, the most attractive figure in literary history," was imperfect in his mastery of the best ideas current in his time and—a graver defect—the victim of a melancholy which blinded him to elements of permanent and essential significance in man and his world. Lucretius, far more of a thinker than either Horace or Vergil, is the victim of excessive thought. He is another Empedocles. In a sentence which links Arnold's standard of spiritual values in this, the first of his essays in literary criticism, with the code of *Empedocles on Etna*, "The Scholar Gipsy," and other poems he observes: "The predominance of thought, of reflection, in modern epochs, is not without its penalties; in the unsound, in the over-tasked, in the over-sensitive, it has produced the most painful, the most lamentable results; it has produced a state of feeling unknown to less enlightened but perhaps healthier epochs—the feeling of depression, the feeling of ennui." Arnold illustrates the feeling of ennui from the close of the third book of the

De rerum natura, quoting the account of a man beside himself with boredom, rushing abroad because he cannot endure his home and rushing home because he has found nothing to interest him abroad. The passage was one that powerfully impressed Arnold, for he was embroidering it almost a decade later in his account of the ennui of the Roman aristocrat in "Obermann Once More":

> In his cool hall, with haggard eyes,
> The Roman noble lay;
> He drove abroad, in furious guise,
> Along the Appian way;
>
> He made a feast, drank fierce and fast,
> And crown'd his hair with flowers—
> No easier nor no quicker pass'd
> The impracticable hours.[4]

Such ennui, with the depression it creates, obscures the vision of Lucretius and twists his judgment. Whether he is contemplating the spectacle of the world about him (as rich as the world has ever offered—richer, indeed) or engaging in self-communion, "he has to keep perpetually repeating his formula of disenchantment and annihilation." The literature of the great age of Rome is not an adequate literature. Its three principal poets (and of the writers of prose Arnold scarcely makes any mention) lack steadiness of vision, serenity, and balance and are therefore incapable of true greatness.

With this literature, disappointingly inferior to the age from which it came, Arnold contrasts that of the age of Pericles in which, for him, the principal literary figure is Sophocles. He repeats the phrase he had used to characterize the excellence of Sophocles in 1849, that he "saw life steadily and saw it whole." The poetry of Sophocles is, he says, pervaded by "the charm of that noble serenity which always accompanies true insight." With such serenity it presents not part of man, as Horace does, but the whole, "human nature in its completest and most harmonious development." His poetry reflects the age in which it was written, not inadequately as the poetry of Lucretius and Vergil does, but with "consummate unrivalled adequacy." It rises superior to any peculiar bias and is tinged with no personal shortcoming. It is poetry such as may issue from the disposition of disinterestedness (Arnold does not here use the word) when that disposition exists in the most eminent degree.

In this first of the literary essays we find the contrast drawn so often in the poetry between the fever of intellect or of passion or of preoccupation with the world, on the one hand, and, on the other, the character of perfect balance, serenity, and clearness. Between the essay "On the Modern Element in Literature" and the more profound of the poems that had preceded it there is no gap. The listeners to Arnold's inaugural, if they were readers of his poetry, cannot have been surprised by anything they heard.

The lectures that followed during the next three years have not been printed, nor are they known to survive.[5] The study of Arnold's literary criticism must resume with the lectures *On Translating Homer*, the first of these delivered on November 3, 1860. Homer had long been for Arnold a chief example of qualities he associated with the disposition of disinterestedness. In the sonnet of 1849 where he ended by attributing the disinterested disposition to Sophocles he began by attributing it in part at least to Homer, the support of his mind in evil times and the "clearest soul'd of men."[6] In 1853 he had claimed for the

Iliad "a juster measure and a happier vein" than he would allow to any other literary work.[7] In 1857, in the inaugural, he had claimed for Homer an even higher poetical power than belonged to Sophocles.[8] It was not until 1860 that he developed such ideas in a careful treatment of Homer, and even then he did not do so with the fulness that one might wish, for his theme was not the story, the personages, or the ideas of the *Iliad* and the *Odyssey* but how to translate the poems into English verse. "My one object," he professes at the outset, "is to give practical advice to a translator."[9]

Arnold conceived of practical advice, as one would expect, in a liberal way. He was persuaded that unless one could penetrate accurately into the spirit of an author, one could never furnish an adequate translation of any work of his. The grossest of all errors in translating Homer was to misapprehend the essence of his spirit; it was Francis Newman's when he missed Homer's nobility. "Homer is never in any sense to be with truth called prosaic; he is never to be called low. He does not rise and sink with his subject; on the contrary his manner invests his subject, whatever his subject be, with nobleness."[10] To write with continuous nobleness is to write in the "grand style." It is in these lectures that Arnold makes his first and most suggestive use of this phrase which was to be among the most treasured and most elusive in the lexicon of his criticism. He distinguishes between two species of the "grand style"—the simple and the severe. Homer is the master of the "grand style simple." In saying that the "grand style simple" is superior to the "grand style severe" Arnold reveals once again that discontent with intellectualism which had marked so many of the poems and which appeared again in his treatment of Lucretius in the inaugural lecture.

Both these styles, the simple and the severe, are truly grand; the severe seems perhaps the grandest, so long as we attend most to the great personality, to the noble nature, in the poet its author; the simple seems the grandest when we attend most to the exquisite faculty, to the poetical gift. But the simple is no doubt to be preferred. It is the more magical; in the other there is something intellectual, something which gives scope for a play of thought which may exist where the poetical gift is either wanting or present in only inferior degree.[11]

The discontent with intellectualism is not so strong as it once was, but it is still there. Higher than the works of the intellect Arnold sets the noble simplicity of Homer. To the marks of nobility and simplicity Arnold adds, in his praise, the mark of "ease and sweetness," that is, of serenity, and the mark of measure, that is, of repose and steadiness. "Homer's grandeur," he says in closing the last of the original series of lectures, "is not the mixed and turbid grandeur of the great poets of the north, of the authors of *Othello* and *Faust*; it is a perfect, a lovely grandeur. Certainly his poetry has all the energy and power of the poetry of our ruder climates; but it has besides, the pure lines of an Ionian horizon, the liquid clearness of an Ionian sky."[12]

The praise of Homer is praise of a poet who exemplified the disposition of disinterestedness, who was in secure possession of all its principal traits. What of the strategy of disinterestedness? It had been easy for Arnold to adopt it in the report on his educational mission to the Continent in 1859. Originally intended as an official document of the Education Department, *Popular Education in France*, which occupied his leisure up to the time when in the autumn of 1860 he began to compose his Homer lectures, is impersonal and somewhat weighty in manner. It is a work of description and analysis rather than recommendation and estimate. With *On Translating Homer* and even more with *Last Words*, in which he returned to the subject and dealt with the objections the earlier lectures had aroused, recommendation and estimate are essential. As the need appears for strict prescription and trenchant judgment, the problem of devising and preserving the strategy of disinterestedness arises in an acute form.

One principal aspect of the strategy as Arnold conceives it in critical prose is the disavowal of immutable principles, the substitution for them of an appearance, at least, of extreme intellectual mobility. In the Homer lectures he quotes with unbounded approval what is perhaps the most famous of all descriptions of the disposition of intellectual mobility: "The critic of poetry should have the finest tact, the nicest moderation, the most free, flexible and elastic spirit imaginable; he should be indeed the 'ondoyant et divers,' the undulating and diverse being of Montaigne."[13] Critical principles held to one's bosom as immutable truths are likely, Arnold contends, to come between the critic and the object of his consideration, whatever this may be, and likely to lead him to see it on a bias. Over against the position of the doctrinaire, which he disavows, he sets that of the mind which travels light, "unencumbered" by an excess of "erudition" or by an accumulation of "crotchets" or by a burden of "temper." It must at first appear to the reader, and it was unquestionably intended that it should appear to him, that in asserting a preference for intellectual mobility as against immutable principles, in decrying crotchets and temper and unilluminated erudition, Arnold was not merely preaching and exemplifying a devotion to the strategy of disinterestedness but preaching and exemplifying a devotion to the disposition itself.

His conduct of the argument in *On Translating Homer* is very far from that which one would expect in an author devoted to the disposition of disinterestedness. The main theme of the first lecture is that Homer is distinguished by four qualities and that all his English translators from Chapman down to the egregious Francis Newman have failed signally to render one or more of these qualities. The contention that four specified qualities distinguish Homer is put forward with the most easy and oracular assurance; no careful supporting consideration of the Homeric poetry either precedes or follows it. The defects of the several translators are marked with a measure of severity, yet no systematic effort is undertaken to establish that these defects do in reality exist. If the intellectual structure of this first discourse is looked for, it will be found to have the characteristic features of a dogmatic thinker, those, for instance, of Carlyle's essay on Burns or Ruskin's comparison of Turner with Giorgione.[14] Nor is the dogmatic element in Arnold's thought in the Homeric lectures confined to the general conduct of the argument. They are sown with absolute judgments, which are usually flung at the reader without preliminary argument of any significant fulness or thoroughness. In the very first paragraph of the first discourse two such judgments are offered: that Homer is "the most important poetical monument existing" and that it is "certain" that Homer will be more and more read in future. Neither of these statements is of a sort that a critic should make without adducing arguments in its support.

Francis Newman was wholly right, in his pamphlet[15]

written in rebuttal of the judgments upon his translation of the *Iliad* in which the Homer lectures abound, in fastening upon the dogmatic element in Arnold's thought, the "numerous dogmatisms by which he settles the case against me."[16] On many occasions he thinks it proper simply to shout "No!" where Arnold had shouted "Yes!" or "Yes!" where Arnold had shouted "No!" It is an evidence of unsatisfactoriness in Arnold's controversial method that his adversary can meet an important objection with a remark such as this: "I have alleged, and against Mr. Arnold's flat denial I deliberately repeat, that Homer rises and sinks with his subject and is often homely or prosaic."[17] From argument so conducted no one can profit, least of all the author whose work is under review; and the onus must rest upon the person who initiated the argument in such terms.

It is impossible to resist the conclusion that the intellectual mobility in Arnold's lectures is only an appearance, a device, a part of a strategy. Even as a strategy it is unevenly successful. Still, one is lost in admiration of the rhetorical effectiveness in its use which is to be found in a passage such as this:

I suppose I must, before I conclude, say a word or two about my own hexameters; and yet truly on such a topic I am almost ashamed to trouble you. From those perishable objects I feel, I can truly say, a most Oriental detachment. You yourselves are witnesses how little importance when I offered them to you I claimed for them,—how humble a function I designed them to fill. I offered them not as specimens of a competing translation of Homer, but as illustrations of certain canons which I had been trying to establish for Homer's poetry. I said that these canons they might very well illustrate by failing as well as by succeeding: if they illustrate them in any manner I am satisfied. I was thinking of the future translator of Homer, and trying to let him see as clearly as possible what I meant by the combination of characteristics

[61]

which I assigned to Homer's poetry,—by saying that this poetry was at once rapid in movement, plain in words and style, simple and direct in its ideas and noble in manner. I do not suppose that my own hexameters are rapid in movement, plain in words and style, simple and direct in their ideas, and noble in manner; but I am in hopes that a translator, reading them with a genuine interest in his subject and without the slightest grain of personal feeling, may see more clearly as he reads them, what I meant by saying that Homer's poetry is all these. I am in hopes that he may be able to seize more distinctly, when he has before him my

So shone forth, in front of Troy, by the bed of the Xanthus . . . .

or my

Ah, unhappy pair, to Peleus why did we give you . . . .

or my

So he spake, and drove with a cry his steeds into battle.

The exact points which I wish him to avoid in Cowper's

So numerous seemed those fires the banks between . . . .

or in Pope's

Unhappy coursers of immortal strain . . . .

or in Mr. Newman's

He spake and yelling held a-front his single-hoofed horses.

At the same time there may be innumerable points in mine which he ought to avoid also. Of the merit of his own compositions no composer can be admitted the judge.[18]

The practiced rhetorician is everywhere: he is reluctant to speak of such trifles as his own carefully wrought examples; they have no place in his affections—he can view them with the contemplative tranquillity of an eastern sage withdrawn from all possessive interests and exempt from egoistic feelings; they had never been important to his general argument; what role in that argument they had they could satisfy in their shortcomings as well as in their successes: they have none, indeed, of the virtues to be found in the Homeric original; they only point the way toward such virtues; nor do they point the way only to these virtues but also to errors deriving from the translator's spirit; and as the author's own compositions they are not within the range of his clear vision. Such a tissue of apologies and uncertainties must leave an effect of modesty and mobility of spirit.

The passage disarms the reader, as it was intended to do. Intellectually it is a farrago. Arnold begins by claiming an absolute detachment from his hexameters, and he ends by saying that he cannot be a qualified judge of them; but in between he asserts that they fulfil their assigned function and that they have a salutary value in leading the reader to distrust the translations of others. They are not credited with possessing the Homeric virtues, but they nevertheless point the way toward them and must therefore, one would suppose, participate in them. They point the way toward the Homeric virtues, but they may very well point the way to qualities unlike, and therefore possibly inconsistent with, them. The manner of statement here is wholly unlike the substance stated. One may be reminded of a character in a novel Arnold was unaccountably slow to read.[19] It is when Uriah Heep is most intent upon gaining the upper hand that his language and deportment fall into the utmost depths of the humble. "And having such a knowledge of our own umbleness, we must really take care that we're not pushed to the wall by them as isn't umble."

The passage is in fact ironical, with that subtlest kind of irony in which the effect sought is that the reader—at least the usual reader—will not detect the note of irony, which the author is left to enjoy by himself or in the company of a few. Such secret irony is relatively rare in the book. In the more controversial parts of the argument, irony is one of the principal weapons by which Arnold exercises the strategy of disinterestedness; but the irony is overt. It often takes the form of mock self-depreciation, a trait of Arnold's controversial manner which was to persist. Newman, he says, with the "supercilious persiflage" of which T. S. Omond complains, "ends by saying that my ignorance is great. Alas! that is very true. Much as Mr. Newman was mistaken when he talked of my rancour, he is entirely right when he talks of my ignorance. And yet, perverse as it may seem to say so, I sometimes find myself wishing, when dealing with these matters of poetical criticism, that my ignorance were even greater than it is."[20] What a disinterested way of implying his judgment that Newman's pedantic learning was one of the defective means by which he had concocted a translation so appallingly improper. Arnold's judgment is successfully communicated, but by the rhetoric of irony he seems to be an Olympian judge pronouncing that in the case of Francis Newman versus Matthew Arnold the ignorance of one was blameless, the erudition of the other noxious.

Powerful impulses in Arnold are in conflict with the exercise of the disinterested strategy in critical prose. Along with the impulse to dogmatic statement, he has the impulse to sharp comment upon the shortcomings of individuals. His treatment of Ichabod Charles Wright's translation of Homer led his victim to print a public letter to Alford, the dean of Canterbury;[21] and the treatment was indeed summary and severe. In a parenthesis Arnold dispatches his and another version: "Mr. Wright repeats in the main Cowper's manner, as Mr. Sotheby repeats Pope's manner, and neither Mr. Wright's translation nor Mr. Sotheby's has, I must be forgiven for saying, any proper reason for existing."[22] Insulting as this parenthetic slap was found, it is less galling than such a judgment on Francis Newman's work as comes to end the second discourse:

> This is why I have so long occupied myself with Mr. Newman's version; that apart from all faults of execution, his original design was wrong, and that he has done us the good service of declaring that design in its naked wrongness. To bad practice he has prefixed the bad theory which made the practice bad; he has given us a false theory in his preface, and he has exemplified the bad effects of that false theory in his translation. It is because his starting-point is so bad that he runs so badly; and to save others from taking so false a starting-point, may be to save them from running so futile a course.[23]

In so brief a compass "bad" (or its derivative "badly") crops up six times; "false" comes three times, and its effect is strengthened by "fault"; "wrong" and "wrongness" are also there; and as if a dozen of the terms of outright intellectual reprobation were not enough, the term of supercilious disdain "futile" is brought in to add a closing note of blame. To cast out a literary work with such an emphasis of rejection is to write with "temper"; it is to part from the strategy of disinterestedness. We have come a very long way from the undulant and diverse being of Montaigne's admiration.

II

The ideal of disinterestedness as a disposition of his own spirit was first brought into question when Arnold perceived that English education, primary and secondary and universitary, was in need of radical revision and that he was capable of making a contribution toward the revision which would be unique. His original attitude toward his work in the Education Department was baldly that it offered a means whereby he could satisfy Justice Wightman that his daughter, if she married Arnold, would not live in a garret in Grub Street.[24] Throughout the first decade of his service, the 1850's, his annual reports were those of an observant generous-minded official, faithfully accomplishing his task, suggesting modifications in detail, but scarcely caring to see, certainly not succeeding in seeing, the function of education as a whole, not ready to propose any basic reconsideration either of practice or of theory.[25] The calm manner and objective argument that mark the early reports appear also in Arnold's first venture into political and social criticism, *England and the Italian Question*, a pamphlet of 1859. The argument is set forth with academic precision and order, and the calm, rounded sentences express the urbane temper of the writer.

The first sign of a changing attitude comes in 1861, in the Preface to his report on his first mission to the Continent, *Popular Education in France*. Glancing back at the preceding pages he says:

In all the remarks which I am making I impose on myself the rule carefully to abstain from any attempt to suggest a positive application of them. I do not presume to discuss in what manner the world of facts is to adapt itself to the changed world of ideas which I have been describing. I offer general considerations,—presented, I hope, without offensiveness, as I am sure they have been formed without prejudice—considerations suggested by watching the course of men and classes in this country to the silent reflection of thinking minds. This an isolated individual, however humble, may fairly attempt; more he cannot attempt properly; perhaps the time has not yet come for more to be attempted at all.[26]

These are revelatory sentences, especially when they are read in the light of the essay on "The Function of Criticism." The thinking mind, silently reflecting on the spectacle of men and classes, is of the essence of the disinterested disposition. The profession that one is concerned to show how the spectacle appears, considered as material for the world of ideas rather than for the world of facts, is the strategy of disinterestedness. The significance of the closing phrase, in which urgency is denied, will appear later. But this admirable description of the attitude of disinterestedness introduces an admission that for the moment at least the author proposes to abandon it. One more sentence completes the paragraph:

> But one breach of my own rule I shall here venture to commit, by dwelling for a moment on a matter of practical institution to meet new social exigencies: on the intervention of the State in public education.

What follows is the first of Arnold's many attacks upon the culture of the English middle class and its role in the debasement of English civilization.

If his observation year after year of the middle-class Philistine Dissenter[27] in the role of manager of a Wesleyan school was to be his first stimulus to a more direct and specific criticism, the second came from the institution, in 1862, by his official superiors, of the Revised Code, "that social and political blunder," as he thought it, "concocted in the recesses of the Privy Council office, with no advice asked from those practically conversant with schools, no notice given to those who largely support schools."[28] These phrases from the unsigned article on "The Twice Revised Code" are pointed; others are barbed. Attacking his official superiors, Robert Lowe, who was vice-president of the Education Department, and Ralph Lingen, who was its secretary, he describes one as animated by a spirit which must render his every concession valueless—"a spirit of hostility to the system which he administers and to its fundamental principles"—and the other as registering a "want of love for the very course which such a department is created to follow."[29] The tone is very far from that of disinterested objectivity: there is not even a nod in passing toward that ideal. For the first time in his life Arnold found himself an important part of a limited situation which appeared to him a crisis in the intellectual and social development of England. The sense of urgency which he had so clearly failed to feel in the report on popular education on the Continent is now strong within him. It was his view that the zeal of Sir James Kay-Shuttleworth in organizing national aid for primary education and the sagacity of his old chief Lord Lansdowne in enabling Sir James's ideas to become operative were on the point of nullification. In the behavior of their successors in power he found a species of treachery. Besides, Lowe at least had deviated from the normal practice of British ministers and instead of defending his subordinates in the service had made the inspectors the subject of attack. No doubt Arnold's personal feelings were engaged as never before in the writing of prose. But aside from them, the issue was nothing less than a choice between the older order of Lansdowne and Kay-Shuttleworth by which the common people might at least take the first steps toward a rudimentary civilization and the new order which, cynically with Lowe, despairingly with Lingen, condemned the common people to unenlightened drawer-of-water and hewer-of-wood ignorance. When Arnold wrote, the Code was before the Commons. He was dealing the strongest and most direct blow he could on an issue of urgent practical importance. He was not content, as he had been in the document of 1861, simply to state the facts as experience and "the silent reflection of thinking minds" construed them. He took sides; he became pugnacious; he made a furious raid; he risked being blackened with the smoke of conflict. And all this he did a year or so before he delivered his discourse on "The Function of Criticism at the Present Time."

I have noted that the article was unsigned. It was not collected in any of his books. These are perhaps indications of a wish that other work he was doing, work in literary criticism, should not be approached as he thought that Cobbett's and Carlyle's and Ruskin's works of general criticism had been approached, with suspicion, with reluctance to be convinced.

III

In 1863 Arnold's mind turned very markedly toward religious problems. In November, 1862, he had lectured at Oxford on Maurice de Guérin, and there is more religion than poetry in the discourse; he was led on to compose an article on Eugénie de Guérin, which he finished in the spring of the following year, and this was almost all religion.[30] In June he lectured at Oxford on Heine, and the religious is again a principal element, and in November on Joubert, where it is plainly dominant. Sometime during the summer or early autumn he composed his deeply religious essay on Marcus Aurelius.[31]

Another series of religious articles belonging to the same year furnished a more severe test of his capacity for disinterestedness in religious criticism: the series which opened with his January article on "The Bishop and the Philosopher," a consideration of Colenso of Natal in contrast with Spinoza, continued in the next month with a paper on "Dr. Stanley's Lectures on the Jewish Church," and concluded with a shorter piece, written in the spring but published only at the end of the year, "A Word More about Spinoza."[32] Of these the first is the one in which disinterestedness either as a disposition or as a strategy was most difficult to maintain. Colenso's critical consideration of the Pentateuch and the Book of Joshua appeared in 1862; and to speak of it was to raise the chief religious issue of the time in the very form in which quiet judgment was least likely to be possible either in the critic or in his reader.

In "The Bishop and the Philosopher" the most remarkable aspect of strategy is the formidable group of generalizations with which it opens. An intellectual work should encounter two kinds of criticism, the criticism of those expert in the matter with which it deals and the criticism of those who are concerned with the effect of all intellectual works upon the general structure of culture either in the nation in which the work appears or in the world at large. These are the literary critics; and their main function is "to try books as to the influence which they are calculated to have upon the general culture of single nations or of the world at large."[33] If an intellectual work relates to religion, the literary critic will inquire whether it is addressed to the many who should be edified or to the few who should be enlightened. If addressed to the former, the nature and degree of the edification attained will come up for estimate; if addressed to the latter, the nature and degree of the enlightenment furnished will come up. "So far as by any book on religious matters the raw are humanised or the cultivated are advanced to a yet higher culture, so far that book is a subject for literary criticism."[34] Colenso's study of the Pentateuch has a multiple claim on the attention of the literary critic, for it is addressed both to the many and the few, it has for its main purpose the instruction of both, and incidentally it attempts to edify as well. At the close of his assertion of the principles by which as a literary critic he must conduct himself Arnold announces what his verdict is to be: that the book offers no edification to anyone, no instruction to the few, and such an instruction to the many as will work all harm and no good. The shift in strategy from the Homer lectures to this first piece of religious controversy is extraordinary; no sitting loose to one's principles now but rather strict fidelity to them, application of them with systematic rigor. There is a sense, however, in which the introduction of a set of fixed principles aids the critic in attaining the appearance of disinterestedness. By the aid of these principles his criticism is brought to an appearance of impersonality; the effect produced is that it is by an abstraction repeatedly called "literary criticism," not by the particular critic Matthew Arnold, that Colenso's work is judged.

If in structure "The Bishop and the Philosopher" is one of the least personal of Arnold's essays, nevertheless by the introduction of sharp comments on Colenso's methods, the effect of impersonality is weakened. Even before he has begun his initial task of erecting his frame of principles, Arnold allows himself to remark: "Occasionally, the uncritical spirit of our race determines to perform a great public act of self-humiliation. Such an act it has recently accomplished. It has just sent forth as its scapegoat into the wilderness, amidst a titter from educated Europe, the Bishop of Natal."[35] The acrid tone of that general observation, tellingly, cruelly phrased, recurs at the end of each section of the essay devoted to Colenso. Nor is the irony which flavors the essay bland. Colenso before he took up

[71]

biblical criticism had distinguished himself in mathematics. He was the author of a number of textbooks, in which a large number of problems had been given for pupils to work out. It was perhaps inevitable, it was certainly natural, that when he approached the biblical text, he should have been specially concerned with passages in which numbers, proportions, areas, were involved and that something of that frame of mind which enables a man to devise problems for arithmetical solution should have persisted. The sort of crux which disturbed Colenso, Arnold exemplifies by such passages from his work as this: "*If three priests have to eat 264 pigeons a day, how many must each priest eat?*"[36] That is the sort of problem which might appear in one of the early exercises in an elementary textbook in arithmetic. Other problems are more advanced: "*In an area of 1692 square yards, how many lambs per minute can 150,000 persons kill in two hours?*"[37] Whatever the answer may be, it cannot, says Colenso, be the answer required by the text—1,250. Arnold's irony appears not only in the choice of examples and in the sentences in which after each he points out its bearing in Colenso's argument. It appears in his summation of the arithmetical approach to the Pentateuch and the Book of Joshua:

> Even a giant need not waste his strength. The Bishop of Natal has indeed other resources in his conflict with the Pentateuch, if these are insufficient; he has the overcrowding of the Tabernacle doorway, and the little difficulty about the Danites; but he need not have troubled himself to produce them. All he designed to do for the higher culture of his nation has been done without them. It is useless to slay the slain.[38]

Taking together the massive frame of fixed principles with which the essay begins and the recurrence of harshly ironical statement as it proceeds, the reader cannot but feel that Arnold's method was one almost ideally suited to stir a maximum of controversy and controversy of an acrimonious kind. That it did so we should be able to deduce from the mere title of the sequel "A Word More about Spinoza," even without the evidence Arnold's letters supply about the outbreak of rejoinders and challenges which "The Bishop and the Philosopher" precipitated.[39] "A Word More about Spinoza" is in the nature of a *mise au point*; by amplification and rectification Arnold tries to make plainer the essential sense of what he had said of the philosopher in the essay in which he had coupled him with the bishop. But the true sequel to that first essay in this group is the paper on "Dr. Stanley's *Lectures on the Jewish Church*," which followed it in the next issue of the same magazine.

One problem in disinterestedness which this article raises now appears for the first time in Arnold's prose. Arthur Stanley was his father's biographer, the intimate of the Arnold family, and Matthew Arnold's own friend. How shall a friend write disinterestedly about his friend's book? Arnold had found that his closest friends could write very coolly of his poetry. Clough had coupled it with Alexander Smith's and on the whole had found more to admire in the latter's. John Duke Coleridge had reviewed one of Arnold's poetic volumes with asperity and had even made a moral charge against his friend, that of artful plagiarism.[40] In the article on Stanley there is no evidence of that rigor which Clough and Coleridge, perhaps intent upon forestalling the suspicion of logrolling, had visited upon him. The essay is pure eulogy; and Arnold's correspondence gives no reason to suppose that the eulogy was in any respect insincere. There is but one reservation to his praise for Stanley. The state of religion in Protestant England is described as unsatisfactory, so unsatisfactory that a reshaping of religion no less fundamental than the Reformation is required; and Stanley does not offer such a reshaping. His work may fall short of doing so; but as a contribution to the health of religion in England in the meanwhile it could not be better. If the eulogy is high, it is conducted with extreme impersonality, with complete disinterestedness, except for one delicate reference to Arnold's father in the final paragraph.[41] The essay is what a critic may rejoice to write of the work of a friend when that work gives him immense satisfaction.

The essay is not, however, wholly concerned with Stanley. Colenso is almost as prominent in it as in the preceding paper. The contrast between Stanley, who conducts his work as a liberal and wise clergyman should, and Colenso, who does not, is repeatedly emphasized. Colenso had ignored the obligation resting upon the clergy to edify: enlightenment had been his major aim; and although he made occasional gestures toward the obligation to edify, these were risibly inadequate. Edification had been Stanley's aim, and he had acquitted himself excellently of the obligation to edify; he had communicated enlightenment as well. His work would not belong with Spinoza's, it would not instruct the few; but it would edify the many— and the few, if they would care to read it—and, although to a less degree, enlighten them. Thus Stanley satisfied the demands which literary criticism makes upon that kind of religious writer whose main aim is edification. The structure of fixed principles presented at the beginning of the earlier paper is basic to this one as well. Once again the abstraction of literary criticism is invoked to judge in place of the particular critic Matthew Arnold.

Unfortunately the use of the structure is less logical in the paper on Stanley. It appears far more obviously to be a device in argument rather than a true belief. Among many examples two may suffice. "I do not," Arnold insists, "blame the Bishop of Natal's doctrine for its novelty or heterodoxy—literary criticism takes no account of a doctrine's novelty or heterodoxy."[42] Developing this general statement concerning the irrelevance for literary criticism of heterodoxy in doctrine, he says: "Address what doctrine you like to the religious world, be as unorthodox as you will, literary criticism has no authority to blame you." The purport is unmistakable; but how does Arnold proceed? "Only, if your doctrine is evidently not adapted to the needs of the religious life,—if, as you present it, it tends to confound that life rather than to strengthen it, literary criticism has the right to check you; for it at once perceives that your doctrine as you present it is false."[43] One may well rub one's eyes. Literary criticism must not blame; but it may check; it cannot take account of heterodoxy in a doctrine, but it may qualify that doctrine as false. Just as in the passage quoted to illustrate the gap between substance and appearance in the Homer lectures, here once more there is inconsistency; for to check is to have blamed and to assert that something is false is to have decided that it deviates from what, for the speaker, is orthodox. Another example will prove no less damaging to the logic with which Arnold makes use of his structure of principles. In the earlier paper he had asserted that for the few, for men such as Spinoza, devotion to ideas took the place of devotion to religion. F. D. Maurice drew from the statement the inference that Arnold supposed the few did not need religion.[44] Arnold now comments: "By no means: that is a matter which literary criticism does not try."[45] And a little later he asks the question: "Are these few justified, in the sight of God, in so living?" only to answer it at once with a repetition of the previous general statement: "That is a question which literary criticism must not attempt to answer." These statements bear only one clear meaning: that whether or not a man such as Spinoza may properly live outside the communion of the religious, devoting himself to the life of ideas, is a question with which literary criticism has nothing to do, for it transcends literary criticism. Arnold, however, continues: "Such is the worth of intellect, such the benefit which it procures for man, that criticism, itself the creation of intellect, cannot but recognise this purely intellectual life, when really followed, as justified so far as the jurisdiction of criticism extends, and even admirable." Again one rubs one's eyes. For what is this but a statement that literary criticism does have an opinion, does render a judgment, on the case which was just before removed out of its jurisdiction. It may be suggested that Arnold does recognize a distinction between the manner in which such men appear in "God's sight" and the manner in which they appear to literary criticism and that he thus safeguards his consistency. The suggestion would have little merit, for it is obvious that in the view of a liberal thinker such as Arnold, no one, literary critic or philosophic critic or theological critic, could determine how a man's life will appear in "God's sight." Consistency required that Arnold should leave the question as one on which literary criticism could reach no judgment.

The use of the structure of principles is, then, unsatisfactory. But here as in the earlier paper there is no doubt that reference to that structure does assist in conveying an impression of impersonality. Moreover, the concession that certain questions are not within the jurisdiction of literary criticism, even if the concession is intellectually hollow, assists also in diffusing an impression of disinterestedness. Once again the critic is in appearance recognizing that in the areas where men hold their views with the greatest intensity he is not operating.

The final paragraph aims at an impression of disinterestedness in a manner which is logically incompatible with what has previously been asserted. Arnold closes with a statement of his reluctance to consider the issues of religion. According to his structure of principles religious writings, whether for edification or for enlightenment, fall within the scope of literary criticism: they are among its legitimate subjects; and it has not only the right but the duty to consider them. But in the conclusion his argument in defense of his enterprise in the criticism of Colenso and Stanley is the argument we have already noted in his educational criticism—the argument of desperate emergency:

> Those who ask nothing better than to remain silent on such topics, who have to quit their own sphere to speak of them, who cannot touch them without being reminded that they survive those who touched them with far different power [this is the covert allusion to his father mentioned above] you compel, in the mere interest of letters, of intelligence, of general culture, to proclaim truths which it was your function to have made familiar.

Here he is conceding, or rather he is insisting, that he has been making a raid into territory which is not his and that if he has sinned by doing so he should be forgiven; he has spoken only because of the improper silence of those who are the natural watchmen over the territory. The plea is in complete contradiction with the structure of principles governing this and the preceding paper.

Irony has, of course, no role to play in the sympathetic examination of Stanley's work. Even in the sections of the paper concerning Colenso the irony is rare, and it is never except in one passage so harsh as in the earlier paper. After reciting some of the bishop's arithmetical calculations, Arnold bursts out: "Heaven and earth, what a gospel! Is it this which a 'fearless speaker of truth' must 'burst' if he cannot utter? Is this a message which it is woe to him if he does not preach?—this a testimony which he is straitened till he can deliver?"[46] It is perhaps not surprising, in the light of the many inconsistencies which have been considered already, that immediately after such an outbreak Arnold should alter his manner and write: "I wish to lay aside all ridicule, into which literary criticism too readily falls, while I express my unfeigned conviction that in his own heart the Bishop of Natal honestly believes this, and that he originally meant to convey this to his readers."

In one particular the paper on Stanley is a clear expression of the strategy of disinterestedness. In "The Function of Criticism" Arnold was to plead that a critic should hold aloof from parties. In one of the most sharply ironical passages in that essay he was to write, and we are now very near the time when he was to write it: "Away with the notion of proceeding by any other than the course dear to the Philistines; let us have a social movement, let us organise and combine a party to pursue truth and new thought, let us call it *the liberal party* and let us all stick to each other and back each other up."[47] Arnold's attack on Colenso had been met with the warning that "liberals of all shades of opinion are angry with me for rebuking him," by the implication that one liberal—and clearlyArnold's approach to Spinoza was distinctly liberal—owed it to another liberal to support him. Against such partisan criticism he exclaims in the paper on Stanley in words that would be admirably in place in "The Function of Criticism": "Ah! these liberals!—the power for good they have had, and lost: the power for good they will yet again have, and yet again lose. Eternal bondsmen of phrases and catchwords, will they never arrive at the heart of any matter, but always keep muttering round it their silly shibboleths like an incantation?"[48]

From Arnold's letters during the months when he was at work on the three controversial papers it is clear he was conscious that the strategy he was using was not disinterested. Shortly after the appearance of the first of them he says: "I long ago made up my mind that if one had to enounce views not current and popular it was indispensable to enounce them in at once the clearest and most unflinching style possible."[49] The substance of what he would say, then, in such papers, was to be presented in a manner which would not minimize controversy, would lend itself to controversy. In a fuller statement some months later he repeats what he has said here but makes a significant addition:

To an eminently *decorous* clerical journal my tendency to say exactly what I think about things and people is thoroughly distasteful and disquieting. However one cannot change English ideas so much as, if I live, I hope to change them without saying imperturbably what one thinks and making a good many people uncomfortable. The great thing is to speak without a particle of vice, malice, or rancour.[50]

Perhaps vice, malice, and rancor are terms too stern to describe the fashion in which Arnold had just written of the

bishop of Natal; but if one were a friend or a partisan of
the bishop or shared any of his views, still more if one were
the bishop himself, a particle of malice or rancor might be
less of an irritant than the irony with which his views
were dispatched. Certainly the strokes of that irony would
render the bishop himself, his friends, and partisans, those,
too, who without knowing him, shared his views, less
likely to accept Arnold's critical observations than if these
had been presented with the serene detachment which the
strategy of disinterestedness supposes. The use of irony is
a means of preserving elements of a disposition of disinterestedness in the heat of a controversial discussion; but
when the irony has the harshness of some passages in "The
Bishop and the Philosopher" and of one in the paper on
Stanley, it is at variance with a strategy of disinterestedness. This Arnold came to see before 1863 ended. At the
close of October he writes:

It is very animating to think that one at last has a chance of *getting at*
the English public. Such a public as it is, and such a work as one wants
to do with it! Partly nature, partly time and study, have also by this
time taught me thoroughly the precious truth that everything turns upon
one's exercising the power of *persuasion*, of *charm*; that without this all
fury, energy, reasoning power, acquirement, are thrown away and only
render their owner more miserable. Even in one's ridicule one must
preserve a sweetness and good-humour.[51]

These are the lessons in strategy brought home to him,
certainly by the controversy concerning the bishop of
Natal and probably by retrospective consideration of his
educational writings in the immediate past and of his ex-
change of amenities with Francis Newman. The reasoning
power exercised in the article on "The Twice Revised
Code," the energy and approach to fury in the papers dealing with Colenso, and the acquirement shown in his Homer

lectures neither alone nor together would act upon his readers as he wished to act. Another strategy was needed, the strategy of persuasion and of charm. At last the art of disinterestedness had taken possession of Matthew Arnold. He was ready to write the first series of *Essays in Criticism* to which a short work on another subject was to be the prelude as to mood and manner.

IV

The new mood and manner appear in the series of articles on secondary education which Arnold had begun to write in the summer of 1863 and which he collected in 1864 as *A French Eton: Or Middle-Class Education and the State*. In these papers there are scarcely any barbed words: persuasion and charm are everywhere.[52] The first of them is purely descriptive—two pictures of secondary schools in France, the Lycée at Toulouse and Lacordaire's school at Sorèze in the Cevennes. When with the second article Arnold turned from the picturesque record of facts to the application of facts, he strained toward a manner of charm, in the opinion that, if the English middle class for whom he wrote were to be lured into reading him for intellectual profit and practical change, "prodigies of persuasion and insinuation" would require to be performed. Anything sharp, anything devastating, might alienate the audience he had in view; and to the strategy of disinterestedness he sought to add the disposition of disinterestedness, for he says that he believed that in persuasive and charming writing his inner nature found its true account. That the *French Eton* papers have the persuasive and charming manner he sought for them is in general very evident; but disinterestedness, conceived either as a strategy or as a disposition, is something more than a manner.

As in *Popular Education in France* he found that he must deviate from his principle of abstaining from specific proposals. His approach to a deviation is substantially what it had been in the earlier book. He begins by laying down his governing principle of disinterestedness:

> I have no pet scheme to press, no crotchet to gratify, no fanatical zeal for giving this or that particular shape to the public establishment of our secondary instruction. All I say is that it is most urgent to give to the establishment of it a wider, a truly public character, and that only the State can give this. If the matter is but once fairly taken in hand, and by competent agency, I am satisfied.[53]

And again, as in the earlier work, before the paragraph is closed Arnold has begun to present a proposal; indeed in this case he has presented the essentials of a "scheme." A broad system of scholarships is to be instituted; and a prerequisite for the individual student's eligibility shall be the opening of his school to national inspection. This is original with Arnold: and with it he couples his adherence to another quite specific scheme, proposed by Sir John Coleridge—existing secondary schools should be either strengthened or suppressed, to the end that in every English county there should be a minimum of one secondary school state-supported and comparable in excellence of staff and administration with a *lycée*.

The second paper in *A French Eton*, in which these ideas are advanced, was written but a few months before "The Function of Criticism at the Present Time" was delivered. How is one to account for the discrepancy between the program of disinterestedness in the Oxford lecture and the practice of a criticism on another topic in which striking deviations from the disinterested ideal are excused? Arnold's educational writings, like his educational activity, lie somewhat apart, as yet, from the main line of his intellectual life. There is a sense that literary and general criticism should tell upon one's country gradually and a sense that educational criticism—now that a crisis in education is upon England—should tell quickly. The reading of Arnold's educational writings of the early sixties leaves with one a conviction that, once Arnold has clearly discerned that the crisis in education is but a facet of the general crisis in civilization, all his criticism will lose in disinterestedness both of strategy and of disposition. We have next to see the operation of disinterestedness in his literary and general criticism before the conviction of a crisis in English civilization took possession of him.

CHAPTER FOUR

The Climax of Disinterestedness

WHEN Matthew Arnold held the first series of *Essays in Criticism* in his hand, what appealed to him most powerfully was "the admirable riches of human nature that are brought to light in the group of persons of whom they treat, and the sort of unity that as a book to stimulate the better humanity in us the volume has."[1] It is indeed a gallery of portraits with extraordinary attractiveness and elevation. Here is Maurice de Guérin, the essence of romantic youth taken in its more serious and religious aspect, aloof, intense, melancholy. Beside him is his sister, no less intense, scarcely less melancholy although with a quite untroubled faith, and even more deeply serious and religious. Joseph Joubert belongs with them, an ideal example of an older person, no less refined and delicate, no less intense a spiritual being, but marked also by a high and calm intelligence, an "inborn and constant amenity," which gives to him a balance the younger portraits do not have. Marcus Aurelius, "perhaps the most beautiful figure in history," is of the same tribe as Joubert, spiritual and intellectual at once, with his refinement and delicacy, but with a graver melancholy which links his portrait with that of the Guérins. Heine is the portrait of romantic youth seen in another aspect, without the religion, without the conviction of the primacy of spirit or even of intellect, lined more deeply with doubt and passion, even with evil, but in his more bitter fashion no less

serious and no less melancholy. These five full-length portraits dominate the gallery. The other personages are but
sketched; Chateaubriand, Joubert's friend, for all his his-
trionic postures a man of depth and gravity;Lamennais,
Guérin's master, seen as an indulgent and bland priest;
Antoninus Pius, Aurelius' imperial predecessor and almost
his peer in seriousness and austere goodness; St. Francis of
Assisi, the expression of what was most romantic and attractive in the intensity of medieval religion; Spinoza, the
most powerful intelligence of the group but no less distinguished for soul than for intellect; and at the base of
almost every portrait, for comparison, a little medallion
of Goethe.[2]

Perhaps the most significant fact about the group of portraits is the fact that concerns the present argument—their
resemblance to the human ideals presented in various
guises in Arnold's poetry. Again and again they disclose
those traits which in his quest for detachment the poet
Arnold had drawn with such conviction and such yearning.
Maurice de Guérin is a striking case. The great power in
his writing is in natural interpretation: "the most profound
and delicate sense of the life of Nature and the most exquisite felicity in finding expressions to render that
sense."[3] And in the famous comparison of Guérin with
Keats, which has been the target for so much superficial
ridicule, he explains where the source of Guérin's remarkable power in treating nature must lie. Keats, Arnold says,
was incomparable in his sense for the surfaces of nature
and in his ability to find the expressions which would render them; but Guérin "has above all a sense of what
there is adorable and secret in the life of Nature; for
him she is the *Magna Parens;* his expression has there-

fore, more than Keats's, something mystic, inward and profound."[4] He is at one with nature; in this is the explanation of his ability to express its life. He is exactly like the Scholar Gipsy, who was so much a part of nature that the very blackbirds did not notice his presence, whose only concern with the girls who passed along the road was to give them flowers to adorn them as they danced in the nature rite on May Day. The fulness with which Guérin gave himself to nature was compensated by an aloofness from people. The note of aloofness dominates in the first picture Arnold gives us of Maurice de Guérin, De Marzan's account of his first sight of Guérin in a gathering at La Chênaie on Lamennais's return from a crucial mission to Rome: not even Lamennais could distract De Marzan from Guérin, whom he then saw for the first time. It was not only the handsome and melancholy face; it was Guérin's mood that fascinated him: reserved, holding aloof, "listening, observing, and saying nothing."[5] It is the Scholar Gipsy again, withdrawing from the inn made horrible by the clatter of the smock-frocked boors and waiting in silence and withdrawal of spirit as well as body while the Oxford riders make their way home to the line of festal light in Christ-Church hall.

Guérin had also the essential spiritual characteristic of the Scholar Gipsy: both in his withdrawal from people and in his approach to nature he sought one thing; people could not help him to it but, rather, hindered the pursuit, and nature was a means of ingress into it. No word is so true for what harassed both the Scholar Gipsy and Guérin as Wordsworth's phrase "the burden of the mystery." Guérin withdrew from society and joined Lamennais because he thought the mystery was soluble in his terms; he left Lamennais and became a novice at Ploërmel because he thought it was soluble in terms of the ancient monasticism of the church; he left Ploërmel and sought it as a romantic free thinker, groping for a spirit in nature; and in the end, in his last illness, he returned, foiled, to subscribe to the ancient faith. Through it all he had the Scholar Gipsy's unwavering unity of motive and conduct: his one aim, one business, one desire. Like the Scholar Gipsy's, accordingly, his life has an ideal meaning.

If Guérin is like the Scholar Gipsy, Joubert is like Balder and another incarnation of light who will be mentioned presently. Throughout the essay on Joubert the conception of light is constantly stressed. In his house in the Rue Saint-Honoré he passed, says Arnold, his happiest hours in "a room very high up, and admitting plenty of the light which he so loved—a room from which he saw in his own words 'a great deal of sky and very little earth.' "[6] Arnold quotes him as speaking of an immaterial light with no less enthusiasm: of the chosen few as

spirits, lovers of *light*, who when they have an idea to put forth, brood long over it first and wait patiently till it *shines*, as Buffon enjoined, when he defined genius to be the aptitude for patience; spirits who know by experience that the driest matter and the dullest words hide within them the germ and *spark* of some *brightness*, like those fairy nuts in which were found *diamonds*, if one broke the shell and was the right person.[7]

In his praise of Plato, Joubert again resorts to an image of light: "Plato shows us nothing, but he brings *brightness* with him; he puts *light* into our eyes and fills us with a *clearness* by which all objects afterwards become *illuminated*."[8] In his summing up, Arnold celebrates Joubert as "the most prepossessing and convincing of witnesses to the good of loving *light*"; as having found the *"light"* he sought; and as a result having a "whole body" which "was full of *light*"; as a sovereign example of how the love of light has led to its ideal outcome in which "*light should irradiate* and beatify the whole life of him who has it."[9] In "Balder Dead" one of the recurrent phrases is that Balder was "so bright, so lov'd a God."[10] His brightness could not be obscured even by his transference to the gloomy land of Hela, the "nine unlighted realms." The special mark of Balder's divine beauty was in the rays that ringed his head; and it was appropriate that his body should be consumed in the element of light, in fire, and that as the fire died down

> So with a shower of sparks the pile fell in
> Reddening the sea around; and all was dark.[11]

Everywhere in the poem light and darkness stand in contrast. The spirit of Balder is also the spirit of culture in "Thyrsis." In evoking once more the Scholar Gipsy and linking with him both Clough and himself, Arnold emphasizes the symbol of light: "a fugitive and gracious light . . . . shy to illumine." The signal elm is seen at sundown against the "orange and pale violet evening sky." The rediscovery of the elm, which he had thought destroyed or dead, is the assurance that the immaterial *"light we sought is shining still."*[12]

Joubert is like Balder in another respect, in aversion from controversy. Joubert detested the arena of politics in which ideas are obscured and passions tossed into activity. And Balder was not sorry to have lost his place in Valhalla, for Valhalla was a world in which the delights of the senses, feasting and carnage, blurred the mind and the delights of the coarser emotions, envy and jealousy and tri-

umph, debased the spirit. The passage in which Balder
explains his resignation to Hela's realm might almost have
been uttered by Joubert in the course of one of his critical
meditations:

> For I am long since weary of your storm
> Of carnage, and find, Hermod, in your life
> Something too much of war and broils, which make
> Life one perpetual fight, a bath of blood.
> Mine eyes are dizzy with the arrowy hail,
> Mine ears are stunn'd with blows, and sick for calm.
> Inactive therefore let me lie in gloom,
> Unarm'd, inglorious: I attend the course
> Of ages, and my late return to light,
> In times less alien to a spirit mild,
> In new recover'd seats, the happier day.[13]

In no circumstance would Joubert have been content to lie
in gloom, although so to lie might have seemed less hateful
than some forms of activity, and this is really all that
Balder is saying. Otherwise this is an expression congenial
to Joubert's nature and especially so in the emphasis it
assigns to calm.

The quest for calm which plays so large a part in Arnold's poetry distinguishes in an eminent degree the character of Marcus Aurelius. The impression left by the portrait Arnold draws of him is at once serene and austere:
unlike Joubert, it was not easy for him to be what he was,
and he must be austere where Joubert can be suave and
gracious; but if he was obliged to exercise "constraint"
upon himself and thus was the more subject to "melancholy," the attitude for which he sought and which he in
so large measure attained was one of serenity. It is the
attitude of Iseult of Brittany: like her, Marcus Aurelius
has annihilated egotism, he makes no demands, he is a
triumph of impersonality. His mood and hers will lead to

a "delicate and tender sentiment which is less than joy and more than resignation."[14] Marcus Aurelius bore with the infidelity of his empress as Iseult of Brittany bore with the lifelong glorification of the other Iseult by her husband. Only those who had attained the repression of self, who had accomplished detachment, could so conduct their intimate lives.

Maurice de Guérin, Joubert, Marcus Aurelius—they are all examples of that disposition of disinterestedness which Arnold had sought and praised through so much of his poetry and correspondence. The other characters in the *Essays in Criticism* could similarly be related to his admiration of the ideal of disinterestedness. Unity of aim, generous elevation of feeling, the love of light and of calm, the devotion to nature, the predominance of spirit over all else—these are aspects of the disposition of disinterestedness. By the kind of personages he recommends to his readers, as by the kind that he censures in his calculated asides, Arnold is speaking throughout the volume for the full excellence of disinterestedness.

II

In acquiring or developing a disinterested disposition one must learn, in one of Arnold's famous phrases, to see life steadily and see it whole or, in another, to see things as they really are. Without such vision one will succumb to narrow loyalties and will prize certain ideas, certain forms, certain feelings, far above their real value. One who succumbs to narrow loyalties and thus fails in seeing things as they are, becomes, in another Arnold phrase, provincial. In the choice of his subjects and in the kind of stress he lays in dealing with them Arnold is in *Essays in Criticism* warring against provinciality. In "The Literary Influence of Academies" the warfare against provinciality is open and declared: "The provincial spirit exaggerates the value of its ideas, for want of a high standard at hand by which to try them. Or rather, for want of such a standard, it gives one idea too much prominence at the expense of others; it orders its ideas amiss; it is hurried away by fancies; it likes and dislikes too passionately, too exclusively."[15] The critic who aims at spreading the disinterested disposition will therefore emphasize what his countrymen neglect, will exalt what they depreciate. He will seek to redress the balance, in the old and noble sense of the term, to be a "Trimmer." As early as 1859 Arnold was conscious of such a role: he writes in a letter to his sister "K" of the essential resemblance between the work of Ernest Renan and his own. Renan is the spokesman for morality, for its claims are likely to be taken too lightly in France; Arnold is the spokesman for intelligence, which in England runs an equal risk.[16]

In the *Essays in Criticism* he speaks for intelligence but also for many other values which he considers too little esteemed by his countrymen. The tribute to Oxford with which the Preface closes is an instance of his spokesmanship. The home of lost causes and forsaken beliefs and unpopular names and impossible loyalties must win the favor of a critic who would redress the balance. No one was ever less in favor of putting the clock back; but from every quarter-hour the clock has ever struck there is something to be learned; and what Arnold is saying here is that the present moment is but one of countless moments, and its values are mere "silly shibboleths" to those who are ignorant or contemptuous of the moments that have gone before it. To live wholly in any one moment is to be the victim of provinciality, to be incapable of disinterestedness.[17] The writer whose chief concern is with the books printed in his own language in the current season is not a critic at all.[18]

The motive which led Arnold to speak for Oxford is the same as that which led him to speak so often and with such eloquence for the Roman Catholic church. In "The Function of Criticism" he insists that Bossuet's philosophy of history is as intellectually respectable as Luther's theory of grace and that the reigning pope's stock of ideas is as close to reason as the bishop of Durham's.[19] In "Pagan and Mediaeval Religious Sentiment" he insists that the Roman Catholic church is "eminently *the Church*," the church through the centuries of the past and the church of the multitude in all those ages; and for an adequate correlative for it he suggests the "pell-mell of the men and women of Shakespeare's plays."[20] In the essays on Joubert and the Guérins he approaches Catholic doctrine, Catholic piety, and Catholic rites with poetic insight and historical respect. In the paper on Eugénie de Guérin he draws out a formal contrast between the religious setting of Eugénie and that of a Miss Emma Tatham of Margate. Eugénie's devotional associations were with the saints, fine and high spirits in many ages and many countries; Emma Tatham's were with "young female teachers belonging to the Sunday school" and with "Mr. Thomas Rowe, a venerable class-leader." Eugénie's spiritual life was lighted by a moss chapel at Easter and a crib at Christmas; Emma Tatham's was confined by "the bare blank narrowly English setting of . . . . union in church-fellowship with the worshippers at Hawley-Square Chapel, Margate." And he concludes that the want of grace and charm, of spaciousness and history, in the spiritual life of the English girl is no trifle but a "real weakness" and one highly characteristic of the religious life in England.[21]

The constant praise of France is another of Arnold's efforts to enlarge the mental and spiritual horizon of his countrymen. In "The Function of Criticism" he asserts that the great lasting fruit of the French Revolution is that in France the common people are more fully alive than in any other European country.[22] In "The Literary Influence of Academies" he asserts that French literature in the eighteenth century was "the greatest European force" of the time and one of the most powerful intellectual agencies that have ever existed, while the English literature of the age was "provincial and second-rate."[23] In the paper on Maurice de Guérin he asserts that the society which gathered about Lamennais is to the English reader "a most instructive spectacle," for it exhibits—what is a condition of national greatness and a condition most Englishmen do not think that France fulfils—the presence of "treasures of fervour, pure-mindedness and spirituality."[24] The paper on his sister develops the imaginative and poetic quality in French Catholicism in terms contrasting with English weaknesses which have already been mentioned. In the paper on Heine, after showing how the poet brought a mind infused with French ideas and methods to bear on German problems, he remarks that in the literature of other countries too, of England for one, the ideas and methods of the French will very soon make themselves powerfully felt and that the critics of 1910 would address themselves to demonstrating how this had come to pass.[25] In the paper on Joubert he asserts that

Joubert could exercise a broader immediate influence than Coleridge because "there is in France a sympathy with intellectual activity for its own sake, and for the sake of its inherent pleasurableness and beauty" for which there is no English equivalent.[26] The book is almost a eulogy of the French mind, French institutions, French religion, French culture, and the French character, as opposed to their English analogues. In the essay on Spinoza, although with significant reservations, Arnold is the spokesman for Jewish excellence; and in the essay on Heine, again with qualifications, for German as well as for Jewish. A similar motive will appear in his next work of literary criticism, the lectures on Celtic literature.

In more purely literary terms Arnold is seeking to redress a balance by speaking for the importance of form. He envies the French their respect of the mother-tongue. The *Times* arbitrarily preferred the spelling "diocess" to the standard "diocese"[27] and such wilful antics are, Arnold says, inconceivable in France. The French Academy is the custodian of the purity of the language; and its long existence and the honor in which it is held are proofs of the national excellence of taste. Joubert's sense of form was perfect, if paralyzing, for he had perceived that "beauty and light are properties of truth, and that truth is incompletely exhibited if it is exhibited without beauty and light."[28] Similarly, in Maurice de Guérin, Arnold discerns a *"passion for perfection"* which made him prefer silence to inadequate aesthetic expression.[29] In his praise of Heine and of Theocritus formal excellence to the point of magical perfection is among the main values to be emphasized.[30]

A critic who is consciously rectifying an error into

which he believes that a generation of readers have fallen becomes in an attenuated sense, to be sure, a victim of provinciality. What he is stressing is not what may be most important in the work under his scrutiny; it is what in the work will be most instructive for the current generation of readers. He is not, accordingly, writing for men in all future times and in all parts of the world. It would have delighted Arnold no doubt if he had known that a great scholar in French literature living in the United States in the early years of the twentieth century would say of his essay on Joubert what Irving Babbitt has said, that it is "one of the best critical essays ever written in English."[31] Still, the central purpose of Arnold's essay was not to merit such praise in such a quarter but to make elements in Joubert's personality, religion, culture, and style operative in Victorian England. One of the most frequently recurring entries in Arnold's notebooks was the counsel of the author of the *Imitation of Christ*: "Always set for yourself a definite purpose" ("Semper aliquid certi proponendum est").[32] It was no part of his conception of the disposition of disinterestedness at the time when he wrote the *Essays in Criticism* that it should condemn one to live in the ivory tower. By avoiding angry controversy, especially in the areas where angry controversy stirs the emotions of one's readers most—the areas of politics and religion— the critic will in the end affect those readers most, will actually affect their opinions of politics and religion most. There lies the justification, in Arnold's opinion, for the indirect and detached approach. The examples he uses for the kind of opinion in which a critic will wish to affect his readers in the end make plain the definite and immediate purpose for which he wrote. The Victorian reader was, he considered, altogether too prone to believe in the excellence of the social and political arrangements of his country. If one said in downright fashion that these arrangements were highly imperfect, the result would be an angry and obstinate insistence on their excellence. The Victorian reader was also, he thought, too smug about the intellectual consistency of his religious creed. Again, the result of downright criticism would be angry and obstinate persistence in error. It would therefore be wiser to illustrate, as Arnold did in "Pagan and Mediaeval Religious Sentiment" and in the paper on Marcus Aurelius, the high and valuable conceptions of religious doctrine and practice held by men of civilizations far removed in time from his own, Roman Catholic or pagan, and to illustrate, as in the paper on Heine, what different political and social arrangements recommended themselves to men of the nineteenth century who, unlike the Victorians, lived in the main stream of modern civilization. It would be an error in strategy to attempt to prove that Marcus Aurelius or St. Francis was wiser in his religion than "Soapy Sam" Wilberforce or that Heine was wiser in his political and social convictions than Lord Palmerston. When Arnold appears to be on the verge of proving something, it is his strategic plan to execute an apparent withdrawal, as when he says in "Pagan and Mediaeval Religious Sentiment," "I wish to decide nothing as of my own authority; the great art of criticism is to get oneself out of the way and to let humanity decide."[33] Or when, after having raised the question whether the moral or social lot of man has improved since the time of Caesar Augustus, whether the poor upon the Aventine were better or worse off than the poor in Bethnal Green or Spitalfields, he appears to bethink him that he is trespassing where he has no license to go and says "These great questions are not for me"[34] before returning to matters that are literary in the narrower sense. If he had not wished to start the question, he would have blotted out the line. He wishes to start it; as he wishes not to impose the answer but to affect his reader in such a way that sooner or later he will propose the Arnoldian answer to himself.

The method is the reverse of dogmatic; it is suggestive and insinuating. Arnold knows what he wishes the reader to believe; he proposes, if possible, to alter the reader's habits of mind so that he will become open to conviction, so that, to use a phrase from "The Function of Criticism," where Arnold is describing the state of Victorian England, he may begin to wear his cloak more loosely; and he proposes, moreover, to suggest to the reader what main ideas, if his frame of mind is really receptive, he should welcome, develop, and adopt.

III

The writers whom Arnold examines in the first series of *Essays in Criticism* are not those whom he holds to be the greatest. His four great imaginative writers are Homer, Dante, Shakespeare, and Goethe; and if the list were doubled, the new names would probably be Sophocles, Pindar, Milton, and Molière.[35] A list of his great reflective writers is less of a certainty; but it would include, along with many of the biblical authors, Plato, Aristotle, Cicero, the writer of the *Imitation of Christ*, Bossuet, Burke, and, once more, Goethe.[36] None of those I have named receives more than passing references in the first series of *Essays in Criticism*. Joubert, the Guérins, Theocritus, St. Francis—

these all stand in what for Arnold were the byways of literature; Spinoza is indeed a figure of the highest kind in his opinion, but he approaches Spinoza only on the side of his biblical interpretation; Marcus Aurelius has his deep respect, but Arnold would not set him in the company of Aristotle or Goethe; and if he admits to thinking that Heine was, with George Sand, the chief figure in European literature in the quarter-century following 1830, he was always emphatic that this was an unrewarding quarter-century both in thought and art.

In the essay on Joubert, Arnold distinguishes rapidly among kinds of criticism in terms of their subjects. There is the criticism about writers of true and striking genius whose fame has been in keeping with their powers; the criticism about writers whose abilities fell short of genius but who have won broad fame, in excess of their deserts; and the criticism about writers of true but quiet genius whose recognition has been far below their powers. In writing of those in the first group a critic can do little more than draw attention to himself; it is his personality, not his subject, which will arrest attention: "the interest one's readers receive has to do, in general, rather with the treatment than with the subject; they are susceptible of a lively impression rather of the course of the discussion itself,—its turns, vivacity, and novelty,—than of the genius of the author who is the occasion of it."[37] The same is true in the criticism of the second kind. But in the criticism of the third kind the interest will far more easily settle in the subject: the subject itself is new, and it is "indisputably true that from what is new to us we in general learn most"; in the reading of such criticism there is "a sense of an immediate contact with genius itself."[38] The personality of the critic can properly and naturally be repressed. In the paper on "The Function of Criticism," Arnold returns to the distinction. Here he takes the first and second kinds together and describes them as criticism of judgment; and of the third he says that judgment is insinuated along with the communication of fresh information. In criticism which is purely or mainly the expression of judgment he finds something unsatisfactory; and with it he contrasts criticism in which the judgment "almost insensibly forms itself in a fair and clear mind, along with fresh knowledge," and this judgment is, he says, the valuable one. Hence the critic should make it his general practice to deal in the third kind of criticism, reducing his function from the role of "law-giver" to that of "companion and clue"; he should make it his general practice to be impersonal, disinterested.[39]

IV

The *Essays in Criticism* belong almost wholly to this third kind of criticism. But in his asides, particularly in his comparisons, Arnold practices the judicial kind of criticism; and since these asides are both numerous and striking, they remain with the reader and form an essential part of the experience the *Essays in Criticism* provide. There is the remark on John Stuart Mill in the essay on Marcus Aurelius that his spiritual perceptions were keen enough to enable him to escape from the sterility of utilitarianism but not keen enough to enable him to become a writer of real greatness.[40] There is the remark on Byron in the essay on Heine that apart from his genius "he was an ordinary nineteenth-century English gentleman, with little culture and with no ideas."[41] There is the remark on the

English reformation, "the inferior piece given under that name, by Henry the Eighth and a second-rate company, in this island."[42] Such remarks had been a part of Arnold's method in the Homer lectures. He declares in a letter written when he was composing these that gradually he proposed to speak his mind concerning the defects of English figures and that he would begin, as he did, with Ruskin.[43] Such severe asides inevitably imprint a highly personal stamp upon criticism, and they are wholly inconsistent with the aim of criticism as set forth in "Joubert" and "The Function of Criticism."

Nor are the harsh personal judgments always confined to asides. The original title of the essay on Joubert was "A French Coleridge";[44] and Coleridge is recurrently criticized, often at length. The painful gap between his aims and his achievements and the even more painful gap between his ethical ideals and his conduct are emphasized; and of his character, Arnold, in one of his severest moral judgments, observes that it must inspire not merely disesteem but even repugnance.[45] No evidence is adduced. Harsh personal criticism, some of it later retracted, abounds in "The Literary Influence of Academies." When the idea of this paper occurred to him, Arnold was conscious that it would arouse controversy and spoke of it as one of the last controversial writings he would publish.[46] It is not surprising, therefore, that this paper should in method lie somewhat apart from the others in the collection, that its strategy should resemble that of the early religious criticism. The first part of the essay conforms very aptly to the general character of the *Essays in Criticism:* Arnold is supplying fresh information about the French Academy and his judgments do come in almost insensibly and without the note of personal rigor. When he passes to the middle part of the paper, in which he considers the evil effects on English culture of the absence of an academic authority, and to the closing part, in which he illustrates these effects by an analysis of characteristic English prose styles, he is no longer performing as a companion and clue but speaks as a divinely commissioned lawgiver. He asserts the highly personal opinion that Burke is the greatest of English prosewriters;[47] and, covered by this opinion, he feels free to choose as representatives of English prose style those who have sought rich and tumultuous effects, Burke, Jeremy Taylor, Ruskin, and—among the successes of the immediate moment—Kinglake, the historian of the Crimean War. But as Arnold was to discern very clearly long afterward, there is another tradition and tone in English prose no less distinguished, the tradition and tone of Dryden, Addison, Swift, Hazlitt, and, one cannot refrain from adding, Matthew Arnold.[48] Had he selected his examples from authors in this latter list, his argument would have collapsed. Any cultivated reader must feel ill at ease in reading this part of the paper, must feel that he is under the guidance of an arbitrary and highly personal critic.

The formula of impersonal criticism is also betrayed by the strategy employed in the Preface, which was to undergo such striking change in a later edition. The same strategy that was used in the paper on Stanley—the saying that one will not do such and such and then in effect doing it—is used in this circumscribed space not once but twice. The sharp remark on Ichabod Wright's translation of Homer, Arnold withdraws—and expresses his regret for having printed it. "I will not," he says, "raise a finger in self-defence against Mr. Wright's blows." But in a trice he shifts. "I will not," he says, "even ask him,—what it almost irresistibly rises to my lips to ask him when I see he writes from Mapperly—if he can tell me what has become of that poor girl, Wragg."[49] The unasked question is not only asked but asked with an incomparable emphasis. His more general apology for vivacity of expression is conducted in the same terms. The Preface is couched in the style and composed in the temper of the letters to the *Pall Mall Gazette* which Arnold was so soon to write and which were to be the substance of *Friendship's Garland*. And the style and the temper were as far from the impersonal as Arnold ever moved.

How is one to explain the harshness in Arnold's personal comments? Again and again in his letters he expresses his aversion from controversy; and in a note to the first edition of *Essays in Criticism*, introducing some polemical observations on Bishop Colenso, he asserts: "So sincere is my dislike to all personal attack and controversy that I abstain from reprinting, at this distance of time from the occasion which called them forth, the essays in which I criticised the Bishop of Natal's book."[50] Thirty pages farther on he speaks of another living writer in these terms:

> This is the Corinthian style; the glitter of the East with the hardness of the West; "the passion for tinsel" some one, himself a Corinthian, said of Mr. Kinglake's style "of a sensuous Jew with the savage spleen of a dyspeptic Englishman." I do not say this of Mr. Kinglake's style, I am very far from saying it. To say it is to fall into just that hard, brassy, over-stretched style which Mr. Kinglake himself employs so far too much, and which I, for my part reprobate. But when a brother Corinthian of Mr. Kinglake's says it, I feel what he means.[51]

Surely if there is one word for the tone of that passage, the word is "merciless": it has a clever cat-and-mouse ingenuity beside which the downright devastation of Carlyle and Ruskin is merciful. It is beneath my standards of urbanity and amenity to use language of such gross character, of such blunt effect, Arnold is saying; but, although I should not dream of using it, I shall quote it because the substance it conveys is true. To the bludgeoning force of the language he quotes he adds the further offense of his fastidious contempt. I have selected this passage from a number because it was excised from the second edition of the *Essays in Criticism*. The text is full of such afterthoughts. For another example, he excised at the same time the passage in which, after saying that he will not yield to the temptation to do so, he asks Mr. Wright, the translator of the *Iliad*, what has become of his fellow-townswoman at Mapperly, the child-murdering Wragg. One may draw from the multitude of such afterthoughts concerning passages of severe comment on living persons that Arnold often was unable to judge soundly the quality of his own style and tone. The severe personal comments, the harsh scornful irony, are the effects not only of a conflict in strategy but of a defective sense of art.

There is, of course, a quite different kind of irony, a bland and really playful irony, which enables Arnold to suggest an opinion without seeming to engage his feelings. The opening pages of "Pagan and Mediaeval Religious Sentiment" are an instance of this: the picture of the shelves of divinity in the Reading Room of the British Museum. The tone is set when Arnold says: "I am almost afraid to say what he will find there, for fear Mr. Spurgeon, like a second Caliph Omar, should give the library to the flames." The shelves are dominated by Roman Catholic works, the greatest among them being the abbé Migne's collection of the Fathers: "Majestic in its blue and gold unity, this fills shelf after shelf and compartment after compartment, its right mounting up into heaven among the white folios of the *Acta Sanctorum*, its left plunging down into hell among the yellow octavos of the *Law Digest*." Protestant works have to creep into the crannies that are left: the Library of Anglo-Catholic Theology, "learned, decorous, exemplary, but a little uninteresting"; Calvin's works, "rigid, militant, menacing"; the works of Dr. Chalmers, "the Scotch thistle valiantly doing duty as the rose of Sharon, but keeping something very Scotch about it all the time"; the works of Dr. Channing, "the flower of moral and intelligent mediocrity."[52] This last phrase deviates into harshness; but in the rest of the passage the tone is exactly that which enables the writer to insinuate his criticism without seeming to care passionately or fervently about his beliefs or the beliefs of others. As every reader of Arnold's prose knows, there is a vast amount of such urbane and balanced irony in it; and that urbane and balanced irony is an admirable organ of expression for a writer who wishes to avoid the tone of direct controversy, to keep his feelings reined in, to suggest to the reader, rather than dictate, what he should think. It is a tone which suits both the disposition and the strategy of disinterestedness.

V

The ideas and the methods of the *Essays in Criticism* govern Arnold's next work, the lectures on the study of Celtic literature; they shape its organization, dictate its tone, and give it much of its worth; but here they are brought into the service of an aim which is more precise and more limited. That aim was to produce an immediate effect on English attitudes toward Ireland and Wales and an ultimate effect on English policies toward both these tributaries and especially toward harassed and wretched Ireland. Here and there in the lectures Arnold frankly acknowledges both aspects of his underlying aim. In the closing pages he is perfectly explicit. There he records how in 1849 Sir Robert Peel had proposed acquiring for the British Museum the Stowe Library which was extraordinarily rich in Irish manuscripts and how Lord Macaulay, a trustee of the Museum, had reported against the proposal, saying that there was but one small part of the library worth acquiring, some correspondence concerning the American Revolution. In his foolish opinion Lord Macaulay represented the large body of his countrymen. The English were then, and Arnold thinks that twenty years later they continued to be, ignorant of the Irish past, and in their ignorance they supposed that it was no great thing. Their contempt for the living Irish, without which the English policy of oppression would have been inconceivable, had spread out to include everything that reflected the Irish people, all the centuries of their past as well as their present.[53] In a work of the next decade Arnold was to quote Burke's stinging summary of English attitudes toward the Irish people: "They were looked upon as a race of bigoted savages, who were a disgrace to human nature itself."[54] Arnold did not think that English opinion had undergone much improvement in the two-thirds of a century which had passed since Burke had spoken. A professor of Celtic languages and literature in the University of Oxford, preferably an Irishman and a Roman Catholic of the genius, distinction, and enthusiasm of Eugene O'Curry, might have turned the scales against the gross Philistinism of Lord Macaulay and in the present might help to turn the scales against the persistence in the English people of an attitude of stupid and incurious ignorance and in their government of a policy of contemptuous oppression. In the lack of a professor of Celtic the professor of poetry might contribute something toward the same result. The apologetic tone of one who does what he can in default of a more competent authority is almost constant in the first three lectures. The fourth and last lecture, where, since the topic falls within literary criticism, the manner is bolder, closes with the noble plea: "Let us reunite ourselves with our better mind and with the world through science; and let it be one of our angelic revenges on the Philistines, who among their other sins are the guilty authors of Fenianism, to found at Oxford a chair of Celtic, and to send through the gentle ministration of science a message of peace to Ireland."[55]

The urgency of the time might seem to require a less gradual mode of proceeding: "It needs," Arnold admits, "some moderation not to be attacking Philistinism by storm, but to mine it through such gradual means as the slow approaches of culture and the introduction of chairs of Celtic." The temptations to a more direct and strident approach must be repressed, for "the hard unintelligence which is just now our bane, cannot be conquered by storm; it must be suppled and reduced by culture, by a growth in the variety, fulness and sweetness of our spiritual life."[56] The key word "disinterested" follows hard upon this passage and is in frequent use throughout the lectures. In the first of them Arnold objects to the tendency in Celtic specialists, Irish and Welsh alike, to view their materials as

"warm Celt-lovers or as warm Celt-haters, and not as disinterested students of an important matter of science";[57]
in the second he contrasts the "Celt-hater" Nash, whose
habit of mind was a prosecutor's, with the philologist
Zeuss, whose habit of mind was a true scientist's, describing the difference between them as that which separates
the "interested" from the "disinterested" approach;[58] in
the admirable last paragraph of the last lecture, at which I
have already looked, he pleads that the problems of the
Celtic past and equally the problems of the Irish present
should be studied "disinterestedly."[59]

Arnold is at some pains to persuade his audience of the
perfection of his own disinterestedness. His strategy is
many-sided and impressive. He begins by relating at length
his experiences as a chance spectator at an eisteddfod held
at Llandudno in the summer of 1864. The festival found
and left him such an alien in spirit that many of its aspects
are given as comic. The chief character stood in the street,
garbed in the conventional ugliness of the nineteenth century rather oddly set off by a flowing green scarf; the
wind blew and drowned his voice and powdered his whisk-
ers with dust. The solemnity was then transferred within-
doors, and in the competitions for literary prizes a leading
entry was a prose essay on the dreary and most un-Celtic
theme of punctuality. The audience was chiefly of those
whom an older Celtic author had described as "creeping
Saxons," but their impassivity (natural enough not only
because of their different taste and training but also because
they could not understand a word of Welsh) was matched
by that of the few Welsh folk in the rear of the hall. As the
critic left, it was a pleasure to him to come upon a London
acquaintance fresh from town and to fall into conversation

about the exploits of the Parliamentary session and "the mysterious perfections of the Metropolitan Board of Works."[60]

A lecturer who begins in such fashion must surely be one with his feet squarely planted on English earth; he will not discover fancied beauties or illusory virtues in the literature and character of the Celt. At the end of the second lecture Arnold again reassures his audience of his essential Englishness, with the amusing exclamation: "Why, my very name expresses that peculiar Semitico-Saxon mixture which makes the typical Englishman!"[61] This is the disguise he would wear, but a later generation, knowing more of his biography than most of his hearers could, will see through the disguise, for Arnold's mother was a Cornish Celt, a Penrose on one side and a Trevenen on the other. These are among the simpler of the devices by which he seeks to persuade us of the spirit of disinterestedness in which he approaches his theme. From what was in truth his great disqualification for dealing with it—his complete inability to read either Welsh or Irish—he develops a further assertion of disinterestedness of disposition. The experts, "Celt-lovers" or "Celt-haters," have in general suffered from intemperate assurance, from the fatal propensity to say that what might be so was indeed so, that what might not be so was indeed not so. Crushing examples of this assurance are given us: alternative translations of the same passage which have scarcely a phrase in common; alternative explanations of an allusion in which whole philosophies of mythology are implied, philosophies depending for their evidence on any and everything except the actual evidence of Celtic materials. In the midst of such wild advocates, the victims of unbalanced learning, Arnold stands quietly as a cautious and modest inquirer. "I settle nothing, and can settle nothing," he says, "I have not the special knowledge needed for that."[62] The same tone reappears, and here in the very turns of phrase, when he says: "All I purpose is to point out certain correspondences, not yet, perhaps, sufficiently observed and attended to, which seem to lead towards certain conclusions. The following up the inquiry till full proof is reached,—or, perhaps, full disproof,—is what I want to suggest to more competent persons."[63] The lectures are punctuated with expressions which profess the limits of the speaker's knowledge; nor are these expressions, as one may find their analogues in other works of Arnold, intended to strike us as ironical. The effect which Arnold is setting out to produce is this: in a subject where there is much conflict of opinion, where little is known for sure, where positions are affirmed with heat and violence, Arnold, no expert, but widely read in the translations of the primary materials and well read in the chief authorities, cautious by mental habit, with no dangerous ax to grind, is making to us a careful elementary report.

In the lectures Arnold takes two principal positions: that the Celts are a great race, far greater than the English recognize or have ever recognized, and that they are much more intimately linked with the English than common opinion supposes. Common opinion on the English side he exemplifies in two figures, his father and Lyndhurst, the former lord chancellor then in his old age. Thomas Arnold, his son admits, was never weary of contrasting the English with the Celts: "He insisted much oftener on the separation between us and them than on the separation between us and any other race in the world."[64] In writing to Thomas Arnold's Celtic widow, her son is even more downright. Flowing perhaps from his sense of the utter alienness of the Celts was Thomas Arnold's aversion from them, his being "so full of the sense of the Celt's vices, want of steadiness, and want of plain truthfulness, vices to him particularly offensive, that he utterly abhorred him and thought him of no good at all."[65] Lord Lyndhurst, too, felt deeply estranged from the Irish, whom he described as "aliens in speech, in religion, in blood."[66] But what, Matthew Arnold asks, if the Irish are not such aliens? What if their language is closely related to our own? What if the true account of the English people is that they are predominantly Celtic with a relatively slight superstructure of Saxons and Normans? Their religion was the religion of England for more than a thousand years—of that there is no question. What if many of the purest and most admirable expressions of English genius—the language of Keats and of Shakespeare, the painting of Turner and of Reynolds—are deeply marked with the Celtic spirit? Then, surely, the Irish may no longer be dealt the harsh measure of oppression which for centuries has been their burden and the disgrace of England. To philology, to physiology, to history, and to literature Arnold goes for support of his claim that the links between English and Celts are close. Lest his ardor awaken distrust, he pauses at the very height of his demonstrations to insist that "what we want is to *know* the Celt and his genius; not to exalt him or to abase him, but to know him. And for this a disinterested, positive, and constructive criticism is needed."[67] There is no doubt that he does dispel distrust, that he does preserve the appearance of disinterestedness; but, on the other hand, he does clutch at every shred of evidence he can find to sustain his argument—his dependence on current theories of race must now appear astonishingly uncritical—he is in his heart an advocate for the Celt and not a dispassionate judge. The disinterestedness is one of strategy rather than of essential disposition. He wishes to know the Celt; he wishes no less to exalt him.

The wish to exalt the Celt begins to declare itself in the second lecture. True to his strategy of disinterestedness Arnold begins by citing the opinions of others. There is Thomas Moore who knew not a word of Old or Middle Irish but, when something was told him of the character and mass of the medieval writings of his countrymen, remarked that they "could not have been written by fools or for any foolish purpose."[68] There are the eminent Roman witnesses, Strabo, Caesar, and Lucan, the words of the last-named especially weighty and solemn in their tribute to the spirituality and the wisdom of the early Celts.[69] From the witnesses Arnold turns briefly to the texts themselves, in translation; and the qualities in the extracts he gives amply justify the words of Moore and of Lucan. The more elaborate part of his literary criticism he defers until he has shown how much of what is finest in England has the Celtic mark. This mark he contrasts with the Germanic mark; and if in many other places he has spoken well of the German mind and German culture, here almost everything he pauses over is weakness or grossness. The Celt is exalted by contrast with the German. Notice how Arnold handles the failure in both to produce poetry of the highest kind. The Celt fails because he does not with sufficient power and steadiness observe the nature of man and because he does not with sufficient power and steadiness construct aesthetic wholes. But in Celtic poetry there are

[111]

fragments of singular power and beauty, and in the long works, despite their failure in construction, an air of greatness permeates the whole. The failures are disappointing, but they are not repulsive; and the relative successes have charm. The German fails because of an incurable uncertainty in taste and style; and such failure is more than disappointing, it·is repulsive. As Arnold draws out the contrast, he preserves an air of disinterestedness by alluding to the German success in other arts and in the sciences and to the value Germanic traits have in the building of a nation. But his heart is not in the allusions. Where his heart is appears by the pleasure he takes in repeating his references to one physiological curiosity. The Celt, he says, has the better-developed organs of respiration, the German the larger volume of intestines.[70] And what a delightful idea, he adds in one of his uses of the contrast, was that of the Gauls who inflicted a fine on every warrior who "when he appeared on parade was found to stick out too much in front." The idea would be horrible to a large-intestined race, but "has it not an audacious sparkling immaterial manner with it, which lifts one out of routine and sets one's spirits in a glow?"

VI

In the fourth and last of the lectures Arnold's manner undergoes a subtle change, for now he speaks as a literary critic; and, feeling that he is upon his own professional ground, he relaxes his airs of modesty and caution. In the very first sentence of this lecture the new note sounds. If he were asked whence English poetry drew its turn for style, its turn for melancholy, and its turn for natural magic, he would reply "with some doubt" that much of the turn for style came from a Celtic source, "with less doubt" that much of the melancholy had the same source, and "with no doubt at all" that nearly all the natural magic was Celtic in origin.[71] The note of easy but firm assurance, accompanied by fine discrimination, remains throughout the first two-thirds of the lecture. Looking back over the course he has traveled in this lecture and the one before, Arnold must have felt that his audience might think him too absolute in his severity toward German poetry. He executes an interesting maneuver of a kind well known to the reader of the first series of *Essays in Criticism*. Is it suggested that he has been blind to the merits of German poetry? Well, he considers that German "is our great, our only first-rate body of contemporary poetry" and that the chief function of modern poetry, the interpretation of life, only German poetry has fulfilled.[72] These are tremendous statements; and it may well be supposed that the audience which heard them would dismiss the notion that the man who spoke thus could have a tendency to slight German poetry. But as soon as Arnold has made the second of these tremendous statements, he takes away, in one quiet phrase —its implications would not tell upon the common reader—almost all its force. By German poetry he means only Goethe's poetry. The first statement stands unmodified; but, as was said when Arnold's earlier statement that Heine was, with George Sand, the chief figure in European literature in the quarter-century after the death of Goethe was under review, Arnold had so poor an opinion of the writings of his contemporaries that the praise is of almost pitifully small account. This, of course, his audience or the common reader would scarcely remember.

To speak well of the Germans after having spoken so

well of the Celts served admirably to launch Arnold's final effect, which is one of admonition mingled with encouragement. The English have been presented as a mixture of Celt with German (a Norman infusion is admitted, but on this there is no need to pause, it does not affect the method);[73] and Arnold wishes to rule out the effect of self-congratulation. It was necessary, if he were at once to exalt the Celt and to show the close links between the Celt and the Englishman, that he emphasize Celtic elements in English life and culture and that he adopt toward those elements the tone of high praise. How easy it would be for a complacent Englishman to say that what Arnold's study of Celtic culture meant to him was that, in addition to the Germanic excellences he knew he possessed and toward which the lecturer had naturally been a little severe, a little captious, Arnold had shown him that he had a whole new range of excellences he had barely suspected. A mood of self-congratulation was what Arnold would not wish and what would frustrate the final argument of his lectures. Returning to the height of his disinterested strategy, he asserts that in the fact of mixture there is danger, and in the particular mixture of Celt and German there is promise. There is danger in the fact of mixture, for it blurs the character, divides a person and a nation internally, and tends toward confusion, self-consciousness, and awkwardness, all of them marked weaknesses of the English. But in the Celto-German mixture there is promise, for if the Englishman will only attain a clear consciousness of his Celtic element and encourage the growth of it in himself, he will become capable of excellences far beyond what he now possesses. And he might well begin by founding a chair of Celtic at Oxford.[74]

The Celtic lectures are among the happiest examples of Arnold's use of the strategy of disinterestedness. He was never more persuasive; his manner was never quieter; his tone never less personal. Irony is brought into play very seldom and only on occasions where it lends animation to disquisition or gently plays around obvious error and grotesqueness. Harsh personal comment is almost absent, although Arnold could not repress his perpetual scorn for Macaulay and by yielding to it injures the disinterestedness of the last paragraphs of the series. The balancing of opposites is more delicately managed than in the *Essays in Criticism;* and it seldom leads to an exclusive judgment. But the strategy is not accompanied by the disposition of disinterestedness in its truth and fulness. The preference for "mining by slow approaches" rather than a more direct consideration of the Irish and Welsh problems is a note of the disposition of disinterestedness. The conception of the present as but a moment forming part of a long process is another. But the choice of a subject such as Celtic culture at that anxious time, the profusion of such pointed references as those to the Fenians and Philistines, above all, the wish to emphasize on all important occasions what will exalt the Celt and link him to the Englishman, are expressions of a sense of crisis. They reflect a practical purpose, a policy of reform. *On the Study of Celtic Literature* is in essence a pamphlet, not a treatise or appreciation; but it is a pamphlet in which the argument is conducted with a winning sobriety and calm. The lapses from disinterestedness in strategy are venial; and they are hidden from all but the closest study by the mildness and serenity of the tone.

CHAPTER FIVE

Toward a Practical Criticism

IN THE underlying aim to improve English attitudes and
policies toward Wales and Ireland the Celtic lectures
point forward; but in mood and manner they point
backward to the first series of *Essays in Criticism*. For
clearer indications of the movement toward the position
Arnold was next to occupy, we look to the valedictory
from the Oxford chair of poetry and the report on his second educational mission to the Continent. In *Schools and
Universities on the Continent* (1868), as compared with all
his previous writings on education, a sense of a crisis of
broader area and deeper implications declares itself, along
with a stronger conviction of the role education at all levels
inevitably plays in determining the qualities of a nation's
civilization.

Despite the interruption it would bring to his writing of
poetry and the difficulties it would pose for his performance of his duties in the Oxford chair, it was to Arnold's
deep satisfaction that in the winter of 1865 he was again
commissioned to describe and evaluate Continental aims
and methods in education.[1] The purpose was now to illuminate the problems not of primary but of secondary, and
incidentally of university, education. The area of inquiry
was new to Arnold, for his responsibilities in the Education Department had been confined to primary schools and
the institutions in which teachers for these were prepared.
Perhaps because of the unfamiliarity of the material, the

second report was much longer and depended almost as much on Arnold's readings as on his observations in the course of the seven months he spent abroad. It occupied, as his letters testify, the greater part of his leisure during 1866 and 1867.[2] The result is the most weighty of all his utterances upon education. Inevitably, the body of the book is devoted to description of teaching and administration in Continental institutions of education above the primary level. But even in the chapters of description there are many *aperçus*, in which Arnold passes back and forth between the area of education and the area of civilization, especially in the form of social and political organization in the national unit. If *Schools and Universities on the Continent* is read as a document in the development of Arnold's social conceptions and general beliefs, every chapter has a high interest. Above all, the two substantial concluding chapters are revelatory, for in them Arnold is drawing out in black and white not simply his deductions for the organization of English education but his deductions for the organization of England as a modern and adequate civilization. How natural it had become for him to move from the part to the whole the following striking passage will disclose:

I have now on two occasions, first in 1859 and again in 1865 had to make a close study, on the spot and for many months together of one of the most important branches of the civil organisation of the most civilised states of the Continent. Few Englishmen have had such an experience. If the convictions with which it leaves me seem strange to many Englishmen, it is not that I am differently constituted from the rest of my countrymen, but that I have seen what would certainly give to them too, if they had seen it with their own eyes as I have, reflections which they never had before. No one of open mind, and not hardened in routine and prejudice could observe for so long and from so near as I observed it, the civil organisation of France, Germany, Italy, Switzerland, Holland, without having the conviction forced upon him that these countries have a civil organisation which has been framed with forethought and design to meet the wants of modern society; while our civil organisation in England still remains what time and chance have made it.[3]

Two pages of comment on the elements of anarchy in English political and social organization follow, in which Arnold's interest is not in the shortcomings of education taken by themselves but in the general weakness of the civilization of his nation and the sources of this. He puts two rhetorical questions which come close to what was to be the starting-point of his thinking in *Culture and Anarchy*, which was to be the next of his books: "Who will deny that England has life and progress? but who will also deny that her course begins to show signs of uncertainty and embarrassment?"[4] An acute awareness of such "uncertainty and embarrassment," now arrived at an extreme height, dominates Arnold's thought in the later 1860's. In these same pages occur other ideas which were to be fundamental in *Culture and Anarchy:* the idea that England, for all her energy and progress, is apart from the main stream of thought and life on the Continent, that is, from the modern spirit; the idea that England is an anarchy. It is with evident reluctance that Arnold now quits these general considerations, mentioned so briefly and cautiously in earlier writings on education, remarking, "However on no part of this immense task of transformation have I now to touch, except on that part which relates to education."

II

By 1867 the problem of transforming English education had become for Arnold a crucial aspect of the larger problem of transforming the social and political organization and the civilization of the country. To transform education had long seemed to him urgent; and, aware of his expert knowledge and of how rare such knowledge was, he had become more and more conscious of a very special, a quasi-official, responsibility resting upon him to aid and even to lead in this transformation. The problem belonged to the practical life of the nation; and he had reached the point where he would speak of it not in a disposition of disinterestedness but with the detailed and explicit recommendations and objections which are proper to a practical criticism.

Was there a parallel sense of urgency growing in him concerning the more general transformation? His letters in 1866, 1867, and 1868 make plain that there was. In July, 1866, Arnold and his family were on their balcony overlooking Chester Square in the West End during the evening when the crowd which had rioted at Hyde Park backed into the square and stoned the windows of Sir Richard Mayne, the metropolitan commissioner of police who lived across from them. He reported the circumstance to his mother and told her that the government's mode of managing the issue of reform in the franchise had been "an exhibition of mismanagement, imprudence and weakness almost incredible."[5] He was to remember the spectacle of the rioters when he came to write *Culture and Anarchy* and to suggest resort to the whip, in a vehement passage later suppressed.[6] In December, 1867, the Fenians blew up Clerkenwell Prison, and Arnold was again in London, although not on this occasion in the neighborhood of the outrage.[7] He was to remember it when he wrote the Preface to *On the Study of Celtic Literature*.[8] He at once compared it with the "Hyde Park business."[9] Such outbreaks of violence, along with the weakness in repressing them and in planning for legislation which would avert them by removing the causes, filled him with the gloomiest impressions of the "real hollowness and insufficiency of the whole system of our public life for these many years past, which could not but break down at last, just because it was hollow and insufficient."[10] On the following January 4, in writing to his mother only a few hours after the death of his infant son, it is significant beyond expectation that he should add to the expression of his grief at the bereavement a confession that even at that sad time he suffered also from an "almost painful anxiety about public matters."[11] By January, 1868, if not before, he had discovered in the problem of English social and political organization, conceived in the broadest terms, an urgency no less pressing than he had formerly felt in the problem of English education.

The powerful testimony of his letters is confirmed by Arnold's few political and social writings in 1866 and 1867 and by references to political and social facts and ideas in his other writings. In February, 1866, he printed in the *Cornhill Magazine* his reply to Fitzjames Stephen's criticisms of his social and political attitudes and his methods of formulating them.[12] The appearance of Stephen's paper had led him to examine his conscience and to discover evidence of some disloyalty to the principle of disinterested criticism; and he confesses:

> I had been breaking one of my own cardinal rules: the rule to keep aloof from practice, and to confine myself to the slow and obscure work of trying to understand things, to see them as they are..... I had been meddling with practice, proposing this and that, saying how it might be if we established this or that..... Henceforward let Mr. Kinglake belabour the French as he will, let him describe as many tight

merciless lips as he likes; henceforward let Educational Homes stretch
themselves out in *The Times* to the crack of doom, let Lord Fortescue
bewitch the middle class with ever new blandishments, let any number
of Mansion House meetings propound any number of patchwork
schemes to avoid facing the real difficulty. I am dumb. I let reforming
and instituting alone; I meddle with my neighbor's practice no more.
*He that is unjust, let him be unjust still, and he which is filthy, let him be
filthy still, and he that is righteous, let him be righteous still, and he that is
holy, let him be holy still.*[13]

The passage is astonishing to anyone with an ear for Arnold's prose—and it was to be radically changed before
the article was reprinted in *Friendship's Garland* five years
afterward[14]—it is so ungracious. The attitude assumed
may have the semblance of penitence, the tone is resentful,
even petulant. It is the kind of writing which occurs when
the author is suffering from an unresolved inner tension.
It reads as if it had been written by Ruskin. Revised in
1871, when Arnold had resolved the tension, it was so
vitally changed as to be an appropriate expression of the
regained serenity.

Just after he had delivered the fourth and last of his lectures on Celtic literature, Arnold was invited, in the summer of 1866, to participate in an eisteddfod at Chester. In
declining he wrote a letter which was given to the press
and of which Arnold himself thought sufficiently well to
reprint several paragraphs in 1868 in the introduction to
On the Study of Celtic Literature.[15] The sense of grave political and social crisis in England resounds in these sentences:

We in England have come to that point when the continued advance
and greatness of our nation is threatened by one cause and one cause above
all. Far more than by the helplessness of an aristocracy whose day is
fast coming to an end, far more than by the rawness of a lower class
whose day is only just beginning, we are emperilled by what I call the
Philistinism of our middle class.

Such words as "threatened" and "emperilled" did not drop easily from Arnold's pen in the years before 1866. They reflect that "almost painful anxiety about public matters" which even at a crisis in his personal life it seemed to him natural to emphasize.

From the summer of 1866 to the end of 1867 he gave his time almost wholly to the report which was to issue in *Schools and Universities on the Continent*. He was too pre-occupied by the composition of the report to lecture either in the autumn of 1866 or in the winter of 1867;[16] but his final lecture falling due in the late spring of 1867, he delivered it at the beginning of June, taking as his topic "Culture and Its Enemies."[17] To his Oxford audience on his last appearance he wished to be mild and even conciliatory. "On this the last time that I am to speak from this place, I have permitted myself, in justifying culture and in enforcing the reasons for it, to keep chiefly on ground where I am at one with the central sympathy and instinct of Oxford."[18] But toward the enemies of culture, the Philistines, his tone was mordant. When he speaks of the secular side of the middle class, their worship of the Bitch-Goddess of a commercial society, and says: "Consider these people, then, their way of life, their habits, their manners, the very tones of their voice; look at them attentively; observe the literature they read, the things which give them pleasure, the words which come forth out of their mouths; the thoughts which make the furniture of their minds,"[19] it is as if he were describing the ways of a strange and loathsome insect tribe. And in the parallel passage on the religious side of the middle class he is if possible sharper yet: "Look at the life imaged in such a newspaper as the *Nonconformist*—a life of jealousy of the Establishment, disputes, tea-meetings, openings of chapels, sermons; and then think of it as an ideal of human life, completing itself on all sides, and aspiring with all its organs after sweetness, light, and perfection!"[20] The writer of such passages as these, addressed to the readers of the *Cornhill Magazine* and the general reading public of England—for the words were never altered—as well as to the Oxford listeners, is not using the strategy of disinterestedness; he is not a critic aiming at a slow effect to be achieved initially in the area of general ideas and then carried over by others into the field of practice. This is interested criticism, aiming at immediate effect, composed in a conviction of urgency and intended to be immediately operative as practical comment on issues of practical life. The only limitation upon its practicalness is its negative stress. Disinterestedness as a strategy has ceased to rule in Arnold's criticism; like Cobbett and Carlyle and Ruskin he has begun to write in such terms that what he may say on purely literary and purely speculative topics will hereafter be read by many members of the middle class with a persistent suspicion. He was to discover that this was so.

He ventures into the area where most quickly and most fatally a social critic puts his reputation for detachment in jeopardy—the area of party politics. He eulogizes the spirit of Oxford and as one of its expressions takes the movement of the Tractarians; over against the spirit of Oxford he sets the spirit which fought the Tractarians and inflicted at least a temporary defeat, and defiantly he calls this opposing spirit the spirit of Liberalism. We have seen with what asperity he commented upon the bigots and money-lenders; these are for him the realities of the Liberal party. Liberalism is Philistinism applied to politics.

By linking his attack on a class with the name of a party, he has succeeded in offering a maximum of offense or would do so if he had added, as he fortunately does not, to his eulogy of Oxford explicit praise of the Conservative party. He is not and will never be partisan in the sense of upholding the entire program of a party. Nevertheless he has already passed out of the nonpartisanship, the disinterestedness, which he had celebrated and to which with such uncertain success he had clung. The main questions which take shape in our mind as we read the valedictory with a knowledge of the phases through which its author, now almost forty-five years old, had already come, are these: Will his partisanship, his interestedness, lead him to propose for the general arrangements of English society reforms as precise as he has already proposed for English education? Will he attempt to cling to the strategy of disinterestedness now that he has discarded the disposition? Perhaps a third question may stand with these: Will Arnold appreciate that it is inconsistent with his new point of view to lay claim to the disposition of disinterestedness; will he once and for all put it firmly out of his mind?

III

The argument concerning the quality of contemporary English civilization and the suggestions for its improvement, raised in such newly provocative terms in the Oxford valedictory, were developed in a series of papers on "Anarchy and Authority," appearing in the *Cornhill* in 1868.[21] These papers were Arnold's principal new literary undertaking in that year, the first in which he had been free from the obligation to prepare lectures on poetry. The relation of these papers to the valedictory was so close that in 1869 they were joined with it to make up *Culture and Anarchy*. Most of the papers on "Anarchy and Authority" are more provocative, farther from both the strategy and the disposition of disinterestedness, than the valedictory had been.

They are provocative, first of all, in the abundance of mordant personal comment; and, as happened with the first series of *Essays in Criticism*, the deletions from later editions are evidence of Arnold's inability to judge at an opportune time how sharp his passages of personal comment really were. The significant deletions from the papers on "Anarchy and Authority" did not come when they were revised in 1869 for the first edition of *Culture and Anarchy*. They were deferred until the second edition appeared in 1875. Speaking of these deletions, Professor Dover Wilson attributes them to two motives: the desire to lighten the work of topical allusions, which six years later had lost much of their edge and illumination, and the desire "to remove grounds of offence."[22] The latter was the dominant motive, for Arnold left intact much material, notably in the final chapter, topical in a very high degree but innocent of strong personal animus.

The most interesting example of personal comment later excised is in the second and third chapters. These chapters are the theater of an extraordinary conflict between the interested and disinterested strategies. The guide which Arnold offers to his countrymen for escape from their difficulties is culture; in one of its essential meanings culture is for him the knowledge of the best that has been thought and said; in this best the *Nicomachean Ethics* has a high place; and it is to the *Ethics* that Arnold turns for the method of social analysis he uses in these chapters:

[125]

Having been brought up at Oxford in the bad old times, when we were stuffed with Greek and Aristotle, and thought nothing of preparing ourselves by the study of modern languages,—as after Mr. Lowe's great Edinburgh speech we shall do,—to fight the battles of life with the waiters in foreign hotels, my head is still full of a lumber of phrases we learnt at Oxford from Aristotle, about virtue being in a mean, and about excess and defect, and so on.[23]

By applying the Aristotelian method of analysis to the social conditions of the immediate present, Arnold wins two valuable positions: he exemplifies the value of the guide to life he is recommending, the value of culture; and he makes it possible for himself to treat of the most contentious issues in a tone of disinterested observation and a framework of principles external to his own thought. No sooner has he won this second position than, by the ticketing of mean, excess, and defect in each social class with an individual name, he gives it up. What, for instance, must have been the emotions of the friends and admirers of John Bright's brother Jacob when they read the paragraph in which Arnold complained that, since John was a man of genius, he would not be an appropriate example of the mean of the middle class but that Jacob would do very well; and then, for no clear reason, abandons Jacob Bright for his fellow-member of Parliament for Manchester, Thomas Bazley?[24] The introduction of Jacob Bright into the argument may have a slight rhetorical convenience, enabling Arnold to pass smoothly from John Bright to Thomas Bazley; it is a wanton intrusion of sharp personal comment. This at least, however, may be said for the allusion to Jacob Bright; he was to represent an object of respect, the mean. There is an inevitable modicum of offensiveness in singling any man out to represent an excess or a defect. How must Sir Thomas Bateson, the member of Parliament for Devizes, have felt on discovering in the pages of the *Cornhill* that, while Lord Elcho was the exemplar of the aristocratic mean, he was the representative of the aristocratic excess? To Lord Elcho is ascribed, along with the "high spirit" proper to his class, "ease, serenity, politeness"; but Sir Thomas has far too much of the high spirit which in his character and behavior reaches the height of "impenetrability, defiant courage, and pride of resistance"; and, by implication at least, Sir Thomas is denied all share of "ease, serenity, politeness."[25] In the present text of *Culture and Anarchy* the second and third chapters are almost bare of personal comment; if we are to understand, as Professor Wilson remarks, the "mood"[26] in which Arnold composed the book, we must restore the profusion of personal references.

The conflict between an abstract method of social analysis and a topical stress in presenting the material to be analyzed has a parallel in the work as a whole. On the one hand, in recommending culture as a guide Arnold is praising thought above action, he is saying that what is now needed is the endeavor by calm observation and habitual reflection to see things as they really are. This is to say that he is inculcating a disposition to disinterestedness. In the end the man who has seen things as they really are, will add doing to his seeing; or if the enterprise of trying to see things as they really are turns out to be extremely long and difficult, the man of culture will impart to his pupils and his sons, to the next generation, the outcome of his observations and reflections; and in consequence of his illuminating communications they will act. The trust in culture, in the "mining by slow approaches," as he had called his method in the peroration of the Celtic lectures, supposes that one have qualities which distinguish the disinterested disposition: unity of aim, serene patience in its pursuit, capacity for long-continued, if not indefinite, withdrawal. This is one side of Arnold's thought in *Culture and Anarchy*; the other, to a degree at least a strategy rather than a true part of the thought, is the affirmation that the approach he makes to the problems of the here and now is essentially "practical."

It is clear that among the objections raised to his earlier ventures in social thought the one which now chiefly disturbed him was the charge that he was impractical. The association of his ideas with kid gloves and the pouncet box had become intolerable to him. He was not content to remain in the position he had taken in "The Function of Criticism": that from the point of view of the market place the work of the truly valuable general critic must appear impractical; although, just because it preserves this semblance, it would in the end profoundly affect the essential dispositions of the market place. If the critic were in the clouds, so was the thunderbolt. In 1868 he was absolutely unwilling that his criticism should pass for impractical, even with the Philistines, even in the immediate present. This is the only appropriate construction to place upon the first page of the first of the papers on "Anarchy and Authority," which readers of *Culture and Anarchy* know as the chapter "Doing as One Likes." After he has taken note of the objection and of the widespread demand that the critic propose "practical improvements," he states as his intention "to drive at practice as much as I can by showing the communications and passages into practical life from the doctrine which I am inculcating."[27] To make plain the danger to English civilization that lies in anarchy is to draw from the doctrine of culture "a practical benefit."[28] To discover in the concept of the best self a source of proper authority, with which anarchy may be opposed and in the end subdued, is to make "a contribution in aid of the practical necessities of our times."[29] The same deliberate emphasis on the practical worth of his social thought recurs in the very conception of the final chapter, "Our Liberal Practitioners," in which Arnold sits in judgment on the principal articles in the current program of the Liberal party. In November, 1868, there was to be a general election, and Professor Wilson does not exaggerate in saying that the appearance of "Our Liberal Practitioners" in the *Cornhill* for July and September, just before the dissolution of the House of Commons, was that "almost" of "an electioneering pamphlet."[30] In the strictest sense this chapter is a revelation of the communications and passages into practical life of the doctrine Arnold has been inculcating throughout the papers on "Anarchy and Authority." He is no longer content to treat Liberalism as a concept and to commit to his readers the task of achieving a judgment on the burning immediate issues with which the concept—narrowed and materialized into a program— was facing the country. He will follow the concept into the narrowed and materialized form in which it wakens partisan loyalties and abhorrences of religious intensity. He will begin to write his own *Latter-day Pamphlets*—his "Shooting Niagara—and After."

IV

The culture which Arnold defends against the strictures of its enemies and recommends as the instrument by which the quality of English civilization can be improved and

England saved from the fate of Holland[31] he defines in a highly personal fashion. For him culture is a composite concept. One part of it is the outcome of a wide-ranging curiosity, the "desire to see things as they are," the disinterested disposition, although Arnold does not here make use of the term. The other part of it issues in a desire to translate one's ideas into social realities, to communicate them to a wide audience, to "make reason and the will of God prevail." There is the part of thought, and there is the part of action; in his stress upon the former Arnold is continuing in the position he had tried to hold consistently—but with what limited success has already been seen—in his literary criticism; in his stress upon the latter he is strengthening and enlarging attitudes which had developed in his religious and educational criticism.

A composite concept, when used by a relatively unsystematic thinker, is almost certain to lead to ambiguity. It is exceedingly unlikely that on all occasions on which he uses the word which denotes it he will intend its full composite meaning. Sometimes the full meaning will be intended, sometimes one part, sometimes another part. Not only is Arnold a relatively unsystematic thinker; in this key concept of culture he is bringing together two ideas, each with a long history in his own development, two ideas which have in the course of this development entered into conflict with each other to constitute the main intellectual and spiritual drama of his existence. To note variations in the sense which he now gives to the term "culture" is to illuminate the stage he has reached in his critical attitude, in his intellectual and spiritual development.

When Arnold says "it is no inconsiderable boon which culture confers upon us, if in embarrassed times like the present it enables us to look at the ins and outs of things in this way, without hatred and without partiality, and with a disposition to see the good in everybody all round,"[32] the context, and notably the word "partiality," makes plain that he is thinking of culture as disinterestedness. It is true that one rubs one's eyes at the passage, recalling the author's approach to the money-getting tea-going middle class, to the pride and defiance of Sir Thomas Bateson, to Jacob Bright's total deficiency in the extraordinary qualities of his famous brother. In the approach to these there was no discerning of the good in everybody all round. But we must take the passage as it stands and find there an Arnold who for the moment is purely reflective and disinterested. When only a few pages later in the same paper he speaks of the best self as "the very self which culture, or the study of perfection, seeks to develop in us,"[33] the explanatory phrase shows that his sense is no longer the same: the culture to which he now alludes is not rational but moral. It will not escape us that reposing two senses in one word is of extraordinary convenience in controversial writing. If Arnold were reproached with partisanship, he could reply—as he did—that culture, as understood in the former of these passages, supposed impartiality of view; if he were reproached with dilettantism, he could reply—as he did—that culture required of its votary that, as in the other passage cited, he study to achieve perfection, one's own and that of one's society in general.

When the term culture is intended to carry only a part of its total meaning, ambiguity may be avoided by the addition of a delimiting phrase. Unfortunately the unsystematic Arnold does not always scruple to supply one. When he says that "for resisting anarchy the lovers of culture may prize and employ fire and strength," he makes a statement which can have no appropriateness whatever to the disposition of disinterestedness which is the base for one half of the meaning he gives to culture. Two sentences farther on in the same paragraph he intends, however, the full meaning of the concept when he says: "The true business of the friends of culture now is, to dissipate this false notion, to spread the belief in right reason, and in a firm intelligible law of things, and to get men to allow their thought and consciousness to play on their stock notions and habits disinterestedly and freely."[34]

I do not suggest that in Arnold's use of the key word culture there is real disingenuousness. The fault is rather one of confusion, the gravamen of Frederic Harrison's objection that Arnold lacked "a philosophy with coherent, interdependent, subordinate and derivative principles."[35] He did not perceive, as a strictly logical thinker no doubt would, that the components of his concept were so unlike as almost to be opposed in very principle. He clung to disinterestedness as a disposition, but he strove for practicality also; and he failed to appreciate that he was in fact moving in two directions at the same time.

V

The words "disinterested" and "disinterestedness" which were in such steady use in *On the Study of Celtic Literature* are absent from the papers on "Anarchy and Authority." At many points in the argument they might be expected to turn up; for instance, in the course of the elaborate definition of the Hellenic spirit, so sharply contrasted with the rigidity and partisanship of the Hebraic spirit. The words are almost absent from the Oxford valedictory; their absence from the definition of culture is impressive as evidence of a change in Arnold's view of the function of the critical spirit and indeed in his view of man and his world and the universe which surrounds it.[36]

The disposition of disinterestedness has not been wholly abandoned. It persists, for instance, in Arnold's antipathy to partisanship in the simple practical sense of that term. He has many severe and cutting remarks against the Liberal program, the Liberal party, and the Liberal leaders; but they were not made in the interest of the Conservatives. Stuart Sherman's summing-up of Arnold's view of the two parties is sound:

To the Tory element he devotes relatively little attention. His criticism of them is in general directed at their mental inflexibility and at their indisposition to do anything important. A Tory at the best is a man of sense and some grounding in the eternal verities; but he is disposed to be sluggish, averse to change, hostile to new ideas; he wishes to preserve things as they are; he is content to "muddle along." He is respectable in that he is not the dupe of theorizers; he keeps in touch with realities. What he lacks is vision, generosity, passion for improvement. Many more and much harsher criticisms than these, Arnold utters against the contemporary Whigs or Liberals—not that he loved them less, but that he expected more of them. The liberal movement, in an age of triumphing democracy, was the movement which most needed and invited critical direction.[37]

"I am a Liberal," he professes in the introduction written for the first edition of *Culture and Anarchy*, but his liberalism is not what could satisfy the Liberal party, for he proceeds at once to qualify his adherence to liberalism by saying that it is "tempered by experience, reflection and renouncement,"[38] cautious terms which are in significant contrast to the Liberal slogan of "peace, retrenchment and reform." In 1870 he is happy at the defeat of Liberal candidates because the party had put its trust in false idols.[39]

He is a Liberal, or a liberal, if one prefers, in the sense in which he claims Heine as a liberal—a dissolvent of the *ancien régime*, a soldier in the warfare for the liberation of humanity.[40] Such remoteness from political partisanship is a note of the disinterested observer.

It is reinforced by the disclaimer of political ambition. To the modern reader of *Culture and Anarchy* such a disclaimer sounds superfluous. But Arnold had such political connections as might suggest the possibility of an active career in politics. He had a great Liberal name; and his brother-in-law, William Forster, became Gladstone's vice-president of the Privy Council in 1868 and his lord privy seal in 1870.[41] Matthew Arnold had served for four years as private secretary to one of the senior leaders of the party, "the Nestor of the Whigs," as Lord Lansdowne was called. He had departed from the discretion of a civil servant to oppose his chiefs in the Education Department for introducing a measure which was in essence a cynical derogation from the principles of liberalism.[42] He was, when he wrote *Culture and Anarchy*, only in his middle forties. His disclaimer was vigorous. The House of Commons offers "a Thyestean banquet of claptrap"; to it resort "country gentlemen in search of a club, demagogues in search of a tub, lawyers in search of a place, industrialists in search of gentility." The new forces which were already beginning to shape the future of the country were not, he thought, represented in Parliament: "the centre of movement is not in the House of Commons."[43] The people have an obscure sense that this is so; and the proceedings of Parliament dissatisfy them by their unreality. The disclaimer is strong enough to convince the reader—the middle-class reader, for whom, above all, the work was written—that the author would neither care to make a deal with the Liberals nor go over in a huff to the Conservatives.

But in some circumstances it is possible to be an influential politician without entering Parliament and without strictly identifying one's self with a party. A social thinker who abhors revolution and all forms of the anarchic and who disdains Parliament may well seek the role of a political educator, a pamphleteer. A pamphleteer is scarcely capable of true disinterestedness. Arnold is professing an ambition to be a pamphleteer when toward the end of the work he remarks that the crucial area in contemporary England is "in the fermenting mind of the nation; and his is for the next twenty years the real influence who can address himself to this."[44] Curiously he was to live for exactly twenty years; and it was to this fermenting mind that he was to address *Literature and Dogma*, *God and the Bible*, and the political papers of his final decade. In a letter of 1868 he exclaims: "Plato would have been less perfect than he was had he entered into the stock politics of Athens at his day";[45] but along with this belief he carried the other, announced earlier: "It is very animating to think that one at last has a chance of *getting at* the English public. Such a public as it is, and such a work as one wants to do with it!"[46] He was now taking his place with Carlyle and Ruskin: the term "partisan" applies to their work only in the sense in which it applies to *Culture and Anarchy*.[47]

Arnold's contemporaries would not respect as "practical" a social critic who confined himself to picking holes in the Liberal program for immediate reform. In his educational writings and notably in that one which immediately preceded *Culture and Anarchy*, *Schools and Universities*

on the Continent, he had demonstrated his fertility in
schemes for reform. Now he sounds a note of caution and
prefers to occupy middle ground. He will not take up the
challenge to propose a scheme of positive social reforms to
be set beside the Liberal program of disestablishing the
Irish church, compelling a more even distribution of prop-
erty among the heirs of the intestate, and revoking the ban
on marriage with a man's deceased wife's sister. In the
Preface of 1869 he is explicit in saying that it would be a
radical misconception of the purport of *Culture and Anarchy* to suppose that its author was recommending one set
of positive social reforms as over against the set to which
the Liberal party stood committed. No substitution of one
outfit of machinery for another could possibly satisfy the
needs of the English social crisis. An English academy
could not perform for English civilization services comparable with those for which France was indebted to the
Académie française. It would neither desire, nor be permitted, to do so. The kind of academy that the English
would devise would merely confirm them in their errors.
Machinery in and by itself is unhelpful. As a preparation
for the institution of positive reforms there must be an interval, possibly a very long interval, in which the English
people reflect upon their political and social situation and
see it for what it really is.[48] In the process of seeing their
situation in its true perspective they will require—and
therefore they must now begin to cultivate—an intellectual
disposition which is a form of disinterestedness, a disposition marked by freedom, balance, and elevation. Arnold is
not content with advocating that this disposition be cultivated and then exercised; he indicates and, what is more
important, he emphasizes some conclusions to which its

cultivation and exercise will lead. In doing so he goes far beyond the advocacy of the disinterested disposition and approaches, if he does not enter, the area of "practical" thought and positive reforms.

The habit of reflection with freedom, balance, and elevation must be exercised above all on the concept of the State. Current English thinking about the State was, he believed, anachronistic and otherwise inadequate. It conceived of the State as a power external to the individual, external to his class, restricting his freedom in the interest of something alien to him. Accordingly, an individual or a class was impelled to resist the enlargement of the power of the State, to aim at confining it as narrowly as might be. Pressed to its extreme, such thinking issues in the archdeacon who threatened to throw into his horsepond any inspector from His Majesty's Education Department who ventured into his domain.[49] To such a conception of the State, petrified and noxious, Arnold opposes a conception suggested by a remark made to him in conversation by Jules Michelet—that the French people were "a nation of barbarians civilised by the conscription."[50] By this he takes Michelet to have meant that the ordinary Frenchman appreciated, in consequence of his experience as a conscript soldier, that he was engaged with his fellows from all classes in a common task, required of all in the interest of all. The English people are so far inferior to the French in realistic appreciation of the true role of the State that they would resist conscription as an invasion of their individual liberties. They require to learn that the State is not their oppressor, actually or potentially, but the instrument by which their common interest is most effectively served. The State is the people acting as a corporate unity. Once the English by the exercise of reflection come to this conclusion, they will agree to commit to the State, as they should long ago have done, as much power as will enable it to guard and advance their corporate interest, making it prevail over the interest of any separate group or class.

The exercise of free, balanced, and elevated reflection will lead them to the adoption of a political principle which will be at the base of a reorganization of the national life. If Arnold is not advocating the enactment of a set of positive reforms, he is advocating a principle which, if accepted, will inescapably lead to the enactment of such reforms. He is asking his countrymen to take a step which will lead—as we have in fact seen it lead—to a thousand other steps. If in the strictest sense of the term his suggestion is neither partisan nor practical, it is "interested," since by adopting it Arnold is taking sides, without reservation, in the principal social and political debate of his age. Nor is it possible for Arnold to play down the positive results of adopting his principle of trusting the State; if he were to do so, his social thought would appear all too impractical and would thus lose all chance of making a strong impression on the middle class for whom he was primarily writing.

VI

It is scarcely possible to conceive a problem more taxing to a writer's rhetorical powers, to his powers as a strategist, than the central problem of *Culture and Anarchy*—to persuade the English middle class that it is more fruitful for them to speculate than to legislate and at the same time to persuade them that one's advice is in the highest degree practical. One must offer a model of disinterestedness for their imitation, and one must demonstrate also an impressive familiarity with the surface needs and proposals of the immediate present. It would appear that the solution Arnold devised for the problem was in brief this: he would pulverize the best practical proposals extant for meeting the most apparently urgent national needs; he would suggest that the mistakenness, or at best the absurd inadequacy, of these proposals pointed to the necessity for far more careful fundamental thinking than had yet gone into them; he would demonstrate that culture was the essence of the kind of thinking that was now imperative; and to such a structure of methods he added another contribution which, when carefully considered, is seen to be basically incompatible with at least one part of the structure. This is the recurrent emphasis upon the complete practicalness of all his proceedings, the insistence that stopping just short of presenting a program of positive reforms was at that particular time the proof of a severer realism than producing such a program would denote. Between the role of persuading his middle-class readers that culture was the *unum necessarium* and the role of persuading them that his concept of the State was the essential need for their political and social well-being there was a real incompatibility. It is almost as if the same actor played Hamlet and Laertes and sought to establish that they were but two parts of the same character. In the ultimate duel he would be in an odd quandary; and to exclude the duel would be to pervert the facts. The incompatibility is underlined if one looks in quick succession at short passages in which Arnold is wholly intent on one or other of his two roles. This is Arnold speaking of the intrinsic excellence of culture:

[139]

"Docile echoes of the eternal voice, pliant organs of the infinite will, such workers are going along with the essential movement of the world; and this is their strength and their happy and divine fortune."[51] Here is culture, the instrument of the disinterested disposition, the faculty of the Scholar Gipsy and Maurice de Guérin, of Balder and Heine and Joseph Joubert. It is appropriate—and it is also significant—that as he speaks of it Arnold's style shifts into the poetic prose which he uses to speak of those prophets by whom his youth had been formed, George Sand and Senancour, Goethe and Emerson, Newman and Wordsworth. This is Arnold speaking of his concept of the State as a practical benefit derived from culture: "So that our poor culture, which is flouted as so unpractical, leads us to the very ideas capable of meeting the great want of our present embarrassed times! We want an authority and we find nothing but jealous classes, checks and a deadlock; culture suggests the idea of *the State*."[52] The passages differ as much in substance as they do in style, and one could scarcely say more.

CHAPTER SIX

Re-enactment with Variations

WHAT remains is re-enactment with variations. The pole of disinterestedness represented by the first series of the *Essays in Criticism* and the pole of practical criticism represented by *Culture and Anarchy* both continue to exercise attraction. At times, as in the best among the later literary essays, Arnold is wholly the disinterested critic; at times, as in *Literature and Dogma*, wholly the practical critic. He never attains to rest; no final solution was possible for him. There is, I believe, no virtue in trying to follow the re-enactment of his conflict in all its details; but it is highly interesting to note in the more important and the more revealing of his later works the degree of his oscillation now toward one pole and now toward the other.

In the five years following upon the appearance of the papers on "Anarchy and Authority," Arnold took an ever increasing pleasure in the evidences that came to him of his influence upon the attitudes and opinions of an élite. As a writer of prose he had staked almost everything upon the attainment of influence. His books continued to sell slowly. The first series of the *Essays in Criticism* required four years to reach a second edition; and six years more elapsed before a third was called for. Despite the verve and the multitude of contemporary references in *Culture and Anarchy*, the book waited six years for a second edition. His other works in prose sold scarcely at all.[1] There was the bitterness of truth in Arnold's remark to the Income Tax Commissioners in 1870: "You see before you, gentlemen, what you have often heard of, *an unpopular author*."[2] Just as *Literature and Dogma* was first appearing he could say honestly to the French pastor Fontanès: "Tout ce qui vient de moi s'écoule tres lentement."[3] Still, if his works fell far short of popularity, if they sold in a mere dribble, there was reassurance, and a reassurance of which he now stood in immense need, in the evidence he had that upon key persons his was a shaping influence. In 1869 William Smith, the editor of the *Quarterly Review*, accosting him at a banquet, assured him of forgiveness for the harsh criticism directed at him in the Preface of *Culture and Anarchy* because of the valuable analysis of Nonconformity which accompanied it;[4] the bishop of Derry, a subtle critic of letters, came up to him one afternoon in the Athenaeum and, with the bishop of Peterborough, engaged him in a long conversation, to his evident pleasure;[5] and the year culminated with a dinner party at which Disraeli himself leaned across the table to exclaim: "Sweetness and light I call that, Mr. Arnold, eh?"[6] In 1870 Oxford conferred on him the degree of D.C.L., and his reception by the elder members of the audience astonished him by its warmth;[7] and 1871 brought a letter from one of the true leaders of the younger generation, John Morley, already editing the *Fortnightly Review*.[8] The letter is lost, but we may recapture its substance from Morley's later remarks that Arnold was "the man of letters whom I should like to place in the front line of my generation in serious drift, influence, importance and social insight," and a critic "incomparable among Englishmen of his day."[9] Perhaps the volume of sales did not matter very much: influence was to be won without it.

Between *Culture and Anarchy* and *Literature and Dogma*, Arnold published little. In the four-year interval he records a more varied social life than he had led in the years of his Oxford professorship. Very many of his week ends were swallowed by house parties, and among many complaints at the injudicious use he makes of his time this slightly later outburst to his sister is especially suggestive: "Visiting is the sure parent of idleness. What a frightful waste of time it is."[10] Dinner parties meant late hours; and late hours meant difficulty in rising at six as he was used to do when he had a book or an essay in hand. He lost two sons in 1868; and a third died in 1872. The blows were dreadful for both parents; but if one may read between the lines of the so discreetly edited letters, they had a morbid effect on Mrs. Arnold. She enjoyed nothing so much as sitting by the graves; and there was even a project for moving to Laleham to be near them.[11] Arnold's affection for his wife was deep; and it may be supposed that he passed with her a greater number of his few hours of leisure than he had formerly done. Perhaps the regime of dinner parties and week ends at great country houses was undertaken in a wish to distract her from her grief. The demands of the inspectorship were almost inflexible; and in these years Arnold repeatedly complains of being wasted on work which was not his true business. "It is absurd," he writes to his mother in 1870, "that all the best of my days should be taken up with matters which thousands of other people could do just as well as I, and that what I have a special turn for doing I should have no time for."[12] It was.

There was no new poetry. The only addition to his

[143]

criticism of literature, an essay which was later to take its place in the third edition of the *Essays in Criticism*, was a study of Gobineau's account of a Persian cycle of religious dramas, a faint counterpart to "Pagan and Mediaeval Religious Sentiment," which it now immediately follows.[13] *Friendship's Garland*, published also in 1871, has little that is new; more than two-thirds of its contents had appeared in periodicals before Arnold began to write *Culture and Anarchy*.[14] Another little book, *St. Paul and Protestantism* was the most substantial piece of writing carried out between 1869 and 1873. Published in 1870, it won a larger audience than anything that Arnold had yet written: the second edition was called for within the year.

St. Paul and Protestantism is a sober book. It is a projection of the chapter on "Hebraism and Hellenism" in *Culture and Anarchy*, an attempt to show how the modern Hebraists, the Nonconformists, have inevitably failed to understand aright the text of one of the masters of Hebraism. The subject would have lent itself to ridicule and to the exhibition of a strong bias. Except in the Preface—the essay which was to become in later editions "Modern Dissent"—there is scarcely any ridicule; and the tone adopted in the rest of the book is that of the calm analyst and disinterested historian of religious ideas. The text of Paul should be read "with the sort of critical tact which the study of the human mind and its history, and the acquaintance with many great writers, naturally gives for following the movement of any one single great writer's thought"; it should be read "without preconceived theories to which we want to make his thoughts fit themselves."[15] What is this but to say it should be read disinterestedly? By the Nonconformists it has not been read so. What Paul meant as poetry has been read as dogma; and "prosaic and unintelligent Western readers who have not enough tact for style to comprehend his mode of expression"[16] have twisted passages which have "the character of a chorus of Aeschylus" into the likeness of passages in "a treatise of Aristotle."[17] There is dross in Paul; he had been trained in a school in which the Scriptures were used in an "arbitrary and uncritical fashion, as if they had a talismanic character";[18] and in his Epistles there are chapters which suffer by the use of a scholastic method with its rigid distinctions and glaring unreality. This, his weakness, the Nonconformists have made into his strength; and his strength, the depth and rightness of his religious spirit, they have neglected. In an elaborate analysis of the Epistle to the Romans, Arnold undertakes to show that the weakness, the scholasticism, is secondary and that the strength is primary and unspoiled by what surrounds it. The stress which he sets on the passages which are free from scholasticism is not, he says, a personal one. "The parts of the *Epistle to the Romans* that have occupied us are undoubtedly the parts which not our own theories and inclinations, for we have approached the matter without any, but an impartial criticism of Paul's real line of thought, must elevate as the most important."[19] There is the note of the disinterested manner, and for once we are disposed to say of a complete essay of Arnold that its method and its tone are on the plane of his recommendations for ideal criticism.

In the first edition the long essay on "St. Paul and Protestantism" was preceded by a study, shorter but substantial, of "Puritanism and the Church of England." In it also the method and the tone are generally disinterested;

and the motive is to aid in accomplishing a religious reform by which it may become easier for Englishmen to cultivate the virtues of the disinterested disposition, to achieve "totality of being." A formidable obstacle to the cultivation of disinterestedness in England is the existence of a multitude of sects each claiming either the exclusive possession of Christian truth or at least the possession of an incomparably superior portion of it. The adherents of each sect are narrowed and distorted as human beings; union would allow them a favorable chance of recovering the balance and breadth which a disinterested disposition requires and supposes. But the proposal for union, organic union, which Arnold here advances is an immediate and practical proposal. Arnold quickly discovered that the part of his book in which public interest centered—the part which accounted, too, no doubt, for the demand of a second edition within the year—was the introductory essay. How deeply, in these years between 1869 and 1873, he desired to recover disinterestedness appears in his decision, when the second edition was due, to set the essay on "Puritanism and the Church of England" in a less conspicuous place, "so that the book will no longer have the appearance of making that which was secondary—the part about the Dissenters—primary."[20]

In other prefaces, notably in that to the *Essays in Criticism*, Arnold had shown himself more combative and harsher in irony than in the body of the work. With the Preface to *St. Paul and Protestantism* the phenomenon recurred. A Dissenting member of the House of Commons, speaking on an Education Bill, had exemplified what Arnold most distrusted and disapproved in the Nonconformist temper. "*There was a spirit of watchful jealousy,*" he had said, "*on the part of the Dissenters which made them prone to take offence;* therefore statesmen should not introduce the Established Church into all the institutions of the country." "What a picture," says Arnold; "Good heavens!"[21] A spirit of watchful jealousy, hopelessly at variance with the essence of the Christian spirit, as with the disposition of disinterestedness, advanced now not apologetically, but brazenly, as a reason for deferring to those whom it inflamed! It was too much for Arnold's equability; and his comments had such mordancy that in an edition following the death of the member of Parliament he felt that he should explain that the speech on the Education Bill was not, indeed, a true measure of the abilities of the departed M.P.[22] Elsewhere in the Preface are uncorrected violations of the disinterested manner.[23] Still, in the main, *St. Paul and Protestantism*, like most of Arnold's writing in the period which stretches between *Culture and Anarchy* and *Literature and Dogma*, is quiet work and justifies his saying, as he did a few months after its appearance, that in the "troubled times" whose coming he foresaw he hoped his influence upon his contemporaries would be "healing and reconciling."[24]

II

In 1877 Arnold's successor in the chair of poetry, the elderly mediocrity, Sir Francis Doyle, reached the end of his term. It was suggested to Arnold that Oxford men of light and leading wished that he would come forward as a candidate once more. In declining the suggestion he wrote to one: "If I stood the religious question would be raised, and to have this question raised in an election to a Chair of Poetry would be, in my opinion, a bad thing for the University; to me myself it would be intolerable. . . . . It could hardly be but that the religious question would be raised if I came forward at present, either for the Poetry Chair or for any Chair at Oxford."[25] To another, after his decision had been taken, he wrote: "A theological election for a literary post is an odious thing, and that is what we should have had."[26] Between the poetry and literary criticism of Matthew Arnold and the body of those elder members of the university who had given him their warm applause when he was admitted to the D.C.L. there had fallen a shadow far darker than *Culture and Anarchy* could cast, the shadow of *Literature and Dogma.* When he had first stood for the chair, many of the high Tories had given him their votes, among them John Keble.[27] No one with Keble's opinions could conceivably vote for the author of *Literature and Dogma.* The chair was next occupied by a blameless middle-of-the-road spirit, John Campbell Shairp, who had been among Arnold's undergraduate friends at Balliol. In one of Shairp's lectures from the chair, in the course of a long examination of Arnold's critical principles, there is a suggestive phrase: "Mr. Arnold is never so welcome as when he speaks of poetry and literature."[28]

Shairp did not have it in mind to praise the kind of discourse about literature which Arnold had held in *Literature and Dogma. St. Paul and Protestantism* had its second edition within the year; but five years elapsed before there was a third. There were three editions of *Literature and Dogma* in 1873, a fourth in 1874, and a fifth in 1875. Nor was its success solitary. It appears to have widened very greatly the audience for all Arnold's general criticism, since in 1875 there were new editions of the *Essays in Criticism, Culture and Anarchy,* and *St. Paul and Protestantism.* But if the popularity of *Literature and Dogma* gave to the *Essays in Criticism* a wider audience, that audience would approach the *Essays* not as a series of disinterested criticisms but rather as adumbrations of the controversies over burning issues in *Literature and Dogma*.

In the *Cornhill* in 1871 Arnold had printed two instalments of the work, corresponding to the first hundred and fifteen pages of the text of the book. It is not in this part of the work that offense is likely to be found. The spirit in which Arnold undertakes the delicate task of reinterpreting the Bible in the light of the most modern knowledge is that which he had recommended in key passages of the *Essays in Criticism*.

The valuable thing in letters,—that is, in the acquainting oneself with the best which has been thought and said in the world,—is, as we have often remarked, the judgment which forms itself insensibly in a fair mind along with fresh knowledge; and this judgment almost anyone with a fair mind, who will but trouble himself to try and make acquaintance with the best which has been thought and uttered in the world, may, if he is lucky, hope to attain to. For this judgment comes almost of itself; and what it displaces it displaces easily and naturally, and without any turmoil of controversial reasonings.[29]

Here is the serenity and detachment that had been recommended almost in the same language nearly ten years earlier; and Arnold's practice in the part of *Literature and Dogma* which appeared in the *Cornhill* conforms well with it. Even with the most solicitous delicacy in approach there was a risk in dealing with such a theme in that time and place; but in 1871 he appears to have deferred to the sensibilities of his audience as far as he could without abandoning his essential position. When he stated one aspect of that position, that the miracles of the New Testament record did not really occur, that the account of them is owing to the defective intellectual processes of the New Testament writers or to their misinterpretation of their sources, the *Cornhill* pages were shut against him.[30] Yet in his treatment of the question of miracles in the life of Jesus he studied for as moderate a tone as he could achieve. I assume that the fifth chapter of *Literature and Dogma*, "The Proof from Miracles," was written in the autumn of 1871 and that all that follows it was written later. One cannot be sure; the manuscript is not known to exist; and there are no statements in the letters which are of help at this point. But the general witness of Arnold's letters is that when he wrote for magazines, he was usually toiling at his copy up to the last permissible day and often, indeed, was obliged to request a postponement of an article, even when the article was a part of a series.[31]

At any rate it is in that part of *Literature and Dogma* which follows the chapter on "The Proof from Miracles," and in the "Preface," that the serious deviations from disinterestedness occur. The motive for them is the same as in *Culture and Anarchy* and in the religious and educational criticism of the early 1860's—the conviction of crisis. The Preface opens with a declaration that a revolution in religious belief has become inevitable. The prospect of revolution does not dispense a writer from "the utmost duty of considerateness and caution"; the writer who does not understand that he may do far more harm than good by a proclamation of his opinions at such a time is almost sure to be "a man whose truth is half blunder and wholly useless." This is a promising opening, and it would seem a warrant that studied moderation will be the tone of *Literature and Dogma*. But Arnold quickly turns from the praise of a detached and cautious handling of the crucial religious issue; after concluding the praise of caution by saying that "if the present time is a time to speak there must be a reason why it is so," he says that in truth "there *is* a reason"; and the existence of this reason appears to dispense the critic from all the processes which have been praised and justify him in the most downright approach to the issue.[32] The reason lies in the attitude toward religion in "the great masses of the people" in England. They are, says Arnold, abandoning all religious faith. He quotes a letter from a workingman in which the movement in the masses is said to lie neither toward the evangelical liberalism of F. D. Maurice nor toward the lofty secular ethic of Huxley but toward the militant atheism of Charles Bradlaugh.[33] If the movement is to be arrested in time, there is not a moment to lose. The one means by which it can be arrested, and even reversed, is the freeing of the Bible from the false glosses with which it is accompanied in the beliefs of all Christian groups. To free it from these and to show the power of what remains is the purpose of *Literature and Dogma*.

The critic who sets for himself a purpose such as this will of necessity become contentious: controversy will emerge at every stage in his argument. If he preserves a perfect serenity of disposition, if he studies for the most extreme moderation of manner, it is possible that he may avoid stirring his more orthodox readers into anger or horror. It is possible but not very likely. Arnold does not rest in a moderate manner or in a serene disposition. These two sentences which come early in the Preface will reveal how far short of serenity and moderation he falls:

Our mechanical and materialising theology, with its insane licence of affirmation about God, its insane licence of affirmation about a future state, is really the result of the poverty and inanition of our minds. It is because we cannot trace God in history that we stay the craving of our minds with a fancy-account of him, made up by putting scattered expressions of the Bible together, and taking them literally; it is because we have such a scanty sense of the life of humanity, that we proceed in the like manner in our scheme of a future state.[34]

This is the language of exasperation. So far, Arnold is assailing the theologians of all Christian groups indiscriminately; but as the Preface moves toward its height, the Nonconformists are singled out for special abuse.[35]

The exasperation which appears so clearly in the Preface is also to be found in the later chapters of the book. It is to be found in this sentence on the creeds: "So we have the three creeds: the so-called Apostles' Creed, popular science; the Nicene Creed, learned science; the Athanasian Creed, learned science with a strong dash of temper."[36] Or in this, on the Athanasian Creed, "It is really a mixture,—for true criticism, as it ripens, it is even a grotesque mixture,—of learned pseudo-science with popular *Aberglaube*."[37] Or in this more generalized comment on all theological writings in the Christian tradition:

Learned pseudo-science applied to the data of the Bible is best called plainly what it is,—utter blunder. . . . . To try to tinker such criticism only makes matters worse; the best way is to throw it aside altogether, and forget it as fast as possible. . . . . The hour for softening down, and explaining away, is passed; the whole false notion-work has to go. Mild defences of it leave on the mind a sense of the defender's hopeless inability to perceive our actual situation; violent defences such as Archdeacon Denison's, read alas! only like *"a tale told by an idiot, full of sound and fury, signifying nothing."*[38]

It is in the later chapters only that Arnold makes use of the image of the three Lord Shaftesburys considered in the first chapter of this study. It is in them also that the repeated references to the phrases of the bishops of Winchester and Gloucester in which "unction" was blended with "metaphysics" take the most devastating turns.[39]

In the introduction to *God and the Bible* which appeared in the autumn of 1874,[40] Arnold firmly defends the tone as well as the substance of his references to the two bishops. Samuel Wilberforce, bishop of Winchester, died in 1873, but even his death did not soften Arnold's pen. "Those words of his which we quoted, and his public deliverances far too frequently, had a fault which in men of station and authority who address a society like ours, deserves at all times as severe a check as either blame or ridicule can inflict upon them."[41] Arnold then repeats the phrases on which he had fastened in *Literature and Dogma* not once but almost thirty times:

A man of Bishop Wilberforce's power of mind must know, if he is sincere with himself, that when he talks of "doing something for the honour of Our Lord's Godhead" or of "that infinite separation for time and for eternity which is involved in rejecting the Godhead of the Eternal Son," he must know that by this singular sort of mixture of unction and metaphysics, he is solemnly giving a semblance of conceivability, fixity and certainty to notions which do not possibly admit of them. . . . . And this is claptrap.

The paragraph which follows is, I believe, the most severe in personal comment in all Arnold's writing, and since it appears to be quite forgotten—who now reads *God and the Bible?*—I shall give it in full:

The Times, it is true, speaks of the current Christianity of this country as "an English, a Protestant, and a reasonable religion." *The Times*, however, is a popular newspaper; and the public when it reads there things which suit its wishes, is always half-conscious at least that to suit its wishes they are written. But the late Bishop of Winchester was a man in high office and dignity, a man at the same time of great gifts; he spoke to the English public with authority and with responsibility proportionate to that authority; yet he freely permitted himself the use of claptrap. The use of claptrap to such a public by such a man ought at least to be always severely treated before the tribunal of letters and science, for it will be treated severely nowhere else. Bishop Wilberforce was a man of a sympathetic temper, a dash of genius, a gift of speech, and ardent energy, who professed to be a guide in a time, a society, a sphere of thought, where the first requisite for a guide is perfect sincerity;—and he was signally addicted to claptrap. If by ridicule or by blame we have done anything to discredit a line such as that which he adopted, we cannot regret it. Those who use claptrap as the late Bishop of Winchester used it, those who can enthusiastically extol him as an ideal bishop, only prove their valuelessness for the religious crisis upon which we are now entering. No talents and acquirements can serve in this crisis without an absolute renunciation of claptrap. Those who cannot attain to this have no part in the future which is before us. Real insight and real progress are impossible for them; Jesus would have said of them: *They cannot enter into the kingdom of God.*[42]

To say of a bishop newly in his grave that Jesus will not admit him to heaven—and for an orthodox reader that is the inevitable sense of the passage which closes the attack —is a radical critic's equivalent for a service of excommunication. It is the last resort of an outraged controversialist. Beside it even the dogged insistence on Wilberforce's love of claptrap is anodyne. Arnold's language in the paragraph as a whole is more devastating than even Huxley's famous oral retort to the same bishop a decade earlier.[43]

The exasperation which is so often expressed in *Literature and Dogma* and in *God and the Bible* is but one of the obstacles which prevent Arnold's theological writings from exercising the "healing and reconciling influence" of his original hope. There is another obstacle more formidable. Arnold was wholly sincere—it need scarcely be said—in his belief that in his theological works the negative was secondary, the positive primary. But the negative was grounded in scholarship, the positive was arbitrary and personal. The core of Arnold's positive thought in his dealings with the Bible is very simple: from the fact, forced upon his generation by the careful scrutiny of the Bible by scholarship, that in the text there are inconsistencies, and worse, he draws new strength for the Christian religion. The inconsistencies and worse prove that the scriptural writers were liable to error. If the evangelists, for instance, report of Jesus anything which could diminish his stature, we may remember that "Jesus was far over the heads of his reporters; he is not to be held responsible for their notions, or for all that they make him do or say."[44] How, the reader will at once require to know, may one determine when the thought or conduct of Jesus is rightly reported to us and when misreported? For the New Testament this is the principal problem Arnold had to solve, and his principal problem for the Old Testament was akin to it.

The basis of Arnold's argument is a philosophic assumption that the supernatural does not exist. To this he gave a famous form in the final sentence in the Preface to the popular edition of *Literature and Dogma:* "Our popular religion at present conceives the birth, ministry, and death of Christ as altogether steeped in prodigy, brimful of miracle; —*and miracles do not happen.*"[45] Whenever Jesus speaks in contradiction of this or acts in contravention of this, Arnold assures us that it is not Jesus who speaks or acts, it is the erring reporter who has interpreted a saying or an act in the terms of his limited intelligence. Arnold is ready to run through a chapter of any one of the gospels to point out just when the words and acts of Jesus are truly given and just when the reporter begins a dubious addition to what really was said or done. The reader is brought again and again, by such picking and choosing, as R. H. Hutton calls it,[46] to face the personal philosophy and even the peculiar disposition of the critic. The method is the reverse of a disinterested strategy. It is true that Arnold does provide some principles of interpretation; but despite these, just as the manner of *Literature and Dogma* and *God and the Bible* is impregnated with the personality of the writer, the substance too is highly personal. The total impression left by each of the books is not unfairly summed up in John M. Robertson's phrase concerning Arnold's "imaginary Jesus,"[47] not Jesus but a phantom of him and a phantom whose authorship is unmistakable. More even than *Culture and Anarchy*, much more than *St. Paul and Protestantism*, these books were written for the immediate needs of mid-Victorian England: they were strokes delivered in what Arnold believed to be a crisis in the ethical development of England.

III

If the mood which rules in *St. Paul and Protestantism* has an affinity with that which ruled in the *Essays in Criticism*, the affinity of the mood in *Literature and Dogma* is with that in *Culture and Anarchy*. We have seen the struggle with the middle class which came to its height in *Culture and Anarchy* succeeded by four years of calm in which devotion to disinterestedness as a strategy, and in large measure as a disposition also, reawakened. After the books of biblical controversy came another period of calm.

In January, 1877, appeared in the *Quarterly* an essay, anonymous, as was the custom in that periodical, entitled "A French Critic on Milton." In such inconspicuous fashion Arnold returned after ten years to the criticism of literature. The anonymity is a symbol of the character of the article. It presents not Arnold's summation of Milton but a comparison of Edmond Scherer's with those of Addison, Johnson, and Macaulay. Arnold assigns to himself the detached role of reporter and interpreter. Led on at the close to say a little on his account, he stops short to remark: "I did not propose to write a criticism of my own upon Milton. I proposed to recite and compare the criticisms on him by others."[48] It is the strategy of disinterestedness in its most complete degree. No less revelatory of the mood and purpose is the frequency with which at key points in the essay Arnold makes use of the word "disinterested." "A *disinterested* reader, whose object is not to hear Puritanism and Milton glorified, but to get at the truth about them will surely be dissatisfied" by Macaulay's partisanship and rhetoric. Johnson was "neither sufficiently *disinterested* nor sufficiently flexible nor sufficiently receptive to be a satisfying critic of a poet like Milton." "A completely *disinterested* judgment about a man like Milton is easier to a foreign critic than to an Englishman." Scherer's verdict on Milton is that of a "modern mind *disinterested*, intelligent, sincere."[49] In the study there is very little of Arnold except for the elegance of the arrangement and the exquisite lucidity of the style. Some petulance against Macaulay, whom he still could not mention without loss of his equanimity, alone prevents our seeing in "A French Critic on Milton" a height of disinterestedness in criticism.[50]

It was followed by an essay which is an encomium on a signal example of the disinterested disposition, Lord Falkland, "our martyr of sweetness and light, of lucidity of mind and largeness of temper."[51] The likeness of Falkland to such characters as Joubert and Marcus Aurelius, Balder and the Scholar Gipsy, is very plain. His was the gipsy's country and the gipsy's century. In the last pages the gipsy hovers over the eulogy where Arnold speaks of Falkland and his friends, moderate, reasonable, meditative, retiring, who "by their heroic and hopeless stand against the inadequate ideals dominant in their time kept open their communications with the future, lived with the future," and where he apostrophizes in conclusion the "lime-trees of Tew and quiet Oxfordshire fieldbanks where the first violets are even now raising their heads."[52]

How fully conscious was Arnold's turn away from controversial writing toward purer criticism appears in another document of the same year, the Preface to the *Last Essays on Church and Religion*. The essays belong to 1876, and the last of them to appear in a magazine, "A Psychological Parallel," is singularly free from animus and controversy and abounds in references to its being the author's final venture in religious criticism.[53] In the Preface, Arnold insists that "assuredly it was not for my own pleasure that I entered upon [religious questions] at first, and it is with anything but reluctance that I now part from them."[54] It is through the criticism of literature that Arnold now intends to work, for in literature are to be found the qualities of which contemporary England stands most in need. In the end, by encouraging the development of these qualities, a critic will do his best for religion as for every other aspect of life. The qualities are "flexibility, perceptiveness, and judgment, which are the best fruits of letters."[55] Arnold is now returning to the position he had occupied when he wrote the first series of *Essays in Criticism* and *On the Study of Celtic Literature*, the preference for "mining by slow approaches." Flexibility and perceptiveness are qualities he had always associated with the disinterested disposition.

Among the literary essays of his last decade the one which most perfectly exemplifies the wish to propagate the disposition of disinterestedness by way of literature is "The Study of Poetry," the most important critical statement of Arnold's later years. It is devotion to disinterestedness which leads Arnold to make his plea here for a "real estimate"[56] of a poem, not an estimate growing out of any special appeal the poem may have for one's own peculiar disposition nor an estimate affected by any opinion one may hold of the importance of the poem in the evolution of a form or an attitude but rather an estimate growing out of a perception of its absolute and unchanging beauty and truth. It is of no final significance whether Marot's poetry is at the end of something medieval or at the beginning of something modern or whether Burns's poetry expressed or failed to express adequately the world of "Scotch drink, Scotch religion, and Scotch manners";[57] all that truly matters is the truth and the beauty. The real and the disinterested estimate are the same. The suggestion that in judging any piece of poetry (and Arnold would no doubt say the same of any piece of literature) one should remind one's self of passages in which the absolute and unchanging beauty and truth are intensely, memorably present is an illustration of Arnold's sense of how necessary it is to make one's escape from narrow and distorting responses in terms of the accidents of one's own experience and disposition and to rise to the plateau where one can make his responses unconfined, simply in terms of one's essential human nature. The strategy of the essay is in perfect keeping with the disposition it exalts and is intended to serve: the evolution moves with a spacious ease, and the style has a sober and almost colorless beauty, a perfect unity of texture never once marred by an irruption of petulance or an excess of rhetoric.

Not far below "The Study of Poetry" may be set the almost contemporary essays on "Wordsworth" and "Byron." In the "Wordsworth," Arnold succeeds in maintaining a serenity of temper even in referring to Macaulay. "Lord Macaulay," he says, "had, as we know, his own heightened and telling way of putting things, and we must always make allowance for it."[58] That is all, there is no jab, no obnoxious innuendo. The great excellence of Wordsworth is stated in terms which relate it to the disposition of disinterestedness; his poetry nourishes qualities which are proper to it. By his style when that is at its best, by "his nobly plain manner," and by his substance, which comes from sources independent of any peculiarities of disposition—the great lasting forms of nature, and "the simple elementary affections and duties"— he enables his reader to free himself from prosaic concerns, from the tyrannies of passion and the critical intellect, and to rise to the plane of essential humanity.[59] "Wordsworth tells of what all seek and tells of it at its truest and best source, and yet a source where all may go and draw for it."[60] The essay presented a serious problem in strategy. It was a plea for justice to Wordsworth, and justice meant a higher place than Wordsworth had ever been generally given. There was no earlier critic behind whose adequate praise Arnold could lurk; and on the Continent, to which Arnold had so often gone for the judgment of right reason, he had to concede that Wordsworth was almost unknown.[61] Was it not likely, he must have feared, that his essay would be discounted as the partisan utterance of a Wordsworthian, that it be taken for not a real but a personal estimate? Wordsworth had been a friend of Arnold's father, for twenty years an intimate of the Arnold household, and Arnold himself had known him.[62] About his own personal acquaintance with Wordsworth he is quite frank; he thrice refers to remarks Wordsworth had made in his hearing;[63] and he glances at the friendship between the families when he says at the close: "It is not for nothing that one has been brought up in the veneration of a man so truly worthy of homage; that one has seen him and heard him, lived in his neighborhood, and been familiar with his country."[64] The protection that Arnold seeks against the accusation of partisanship is in the irony with which he speaks of the Wordsworthians, upon the excess of their respect for the philosophic system of the poet and upon their undiscriminating acceptance of his most commonplace poems as mighty utterances.[65] He is thus enabled to conclude with the distinction: "Wordsworth is something more than the pure and sage master of a small band of devoted followers, and we ought not to rest satisfied until he is seen to be what he is. He is one of the very chief glories of English Poetry; and by nothing is England so glorious as by her poetry."[66] Arnold persuades his reader, I think, that he is a discriminating admirer, a safe guide.

For Byron, Arnold's sympathies were imperfect, and in his approach to Byron it is easy for him to convince us that he keeps his balance and discriminates. "I can even remember," he says, "the latter years of Byron's vogue, and have myself felt the expiring wave of that mighty influence, but [I] certainly regard him, and have long regarded him, without illusion."[67] Very much of Byron, both the man and the poet, is surrendered to envious time; but under the mask of the cynic Arnold discerns a great man—greater by far than he had earlier supposed—and under the disguise of the careless craftsman, a great poet. The great man had an instinctive perception of the hollowness in the *ancien régime* which had lingered on in England and thus became, as Heine was to become, a soldier in the warfare for the liberation of humanity.[68] The great poet could cast aside all pettiness and mannerism and nourish himself and his readers on pure beauty, comparable with the beauty in the highest achievements of Wordsworth: "When he warms to his work, when he is inspired, Nature herself seems to take the pen from him as she took it from Wordsworth, and to write for him as she wrote for Wordsworth, though in a different fashion, with her own penetrating simplicity."[69] It is by his perception of sham in the political and social life about him and in the unmannered purity of his style at its best that Byron too serves the disinterested disposition, although he cannot rest in it either as man or as poet.

In such essays as the "Byron," in which Arnold is making rapid discriminations, in which fervid praise is balanced by reservations many and severe, the peculiar charm of the essay on "Wordsworth" is impossible. The short critiques on "Gray" and "Keats," the discourse on "Emerson," are akin to the "Byron." The finest of Arnold's tributes to the disposition of disinterestedness in the years following the "Wordsworth" is the last of his great poems, the elegy on Arthur Stanley composed in the latter months of 1881. More emphatically and above all more picturesquely than in "Thyrsis," he presents his dead friend as light incarnate; light irradiates the poem, sometimes in a mild glow, sometimes in a veritable coruscation. Stanley is set more firmly in the intellectual and spiritual conditions of his time than Clough had been: the light he exemplifies and becomes is a less fanciful light, it is the disposition of disinterestedness as the poet himself has sought to serve it over the long perplexing years:

> Yet in this latter time
> The promise of the prime
> Seem'd to come true at last, O Abbey old!
> It seem'd, a child of light did bring the dower
> Foreshown thee in thy consecration-hour,
> And in thy courts his shining freight unroll'd:
> Bright wits and instincts sure,
> And goodness warm, and truth without alloy,
> And temper sweet, and love of all things pure,
> And joy in light, and power to spread the joy.[70]

Joy in light, and power to spread the joy! this was what he admired in Wordsworth, what he claimed for the great poets in "The Study of Poetry," as it was what he had tried to achieve for his own part early and late.

IV

In the first of Arnold's later literary essays, "A French Critic on Milton," devotion to disinterestedness, both the disposition and the strategy, appears in extraordinary strength and consistency. In the first of his later social essays, "Equality," a performance of the following year, 1878, the devotion is even more impressive. "Equality" was first used as a discourse at the Royal Institution in London where, as Arnold notes, political issues might not be discussed.[71] The restriction does not make him uneasy; on the contrary, he prefers to emphasize how far from the area of practical politics his thoughts have led him. Imagine, he closes by suggesting, Lord Hartington, that pillar of the Liberal party, appearing before his fellow-Liberals in Glasgow and urging them to cease exciting themselves with projects for disestablishment, the breath of their political life, and instead begin to press for legislation to promote equality. It is pure fantasy. "No," Arnold continues, "the matter is at present one for the thoughts of those who think. It is a thing to be turned over in the minds of those who, on the one hand, have the spirit of scientific inquirers, bent on seeing things as they really are; and on the other hand, the spirit of friends of the humane life, lovers of perfection. To your thoughts I commit it."[72] What is this but to say that as a disinterested thinker he has been sharing speculative ideas with an élite, the children of light, themselves disinterested thinkers in an almost equal degree. No action, no step toward action organized or individual, is suggested. The time for the first such step is still distant.

In strategy the discourse is no less impressively disinterested. Arnold begins to build his case against the English religion of inequality by citing the belief in equality or an approximation to it in those other parts of the world where civilization has qualities which demand respect—France, Belgium, Holland, Italy, the French cantons of Switzerland, the Rhenish provinces of Germany, the United States, the British colonies overseas. "You see," he notes, "we are in a manner taking the votes for and against equality."[73] "At present," he says of the movement toward equality in Australia, "I neither praise it nor blame it; I simply count it as one of the votes for equality."[74] Once the votes have been collected, Arnold has to abandon the merely watchful role of the electoral officer; but he continues to efface himself. He reports

some of his own observations at home and abroad and observations made by others and with much sobriety elicits
their bearing upon the problem of what impact equality
and inequality have upon a civilization. The penchant for
the sharp aside, the arrogant or gratuitous condemning remark, does not appear. The style, like that of the literary
essays of this time, is beautifully temperate and transparent.

In the next of the social essays, "Irish Catholicism and
British Liberalism," appearing in the *Fortnightly* for July
of the same year, Arnold finds disinterestedness less easy
to maintain. It was inevitable that he should, for to move
toward a practical solution of the problem of Ireland was
of the greatest urgency. In speaking of Ireland it was
difficult to content one's self with setting afloat some general ideas which in the end might promote an attitude in
the English people from which a policy of wisdom and
justice could issue. A decade earlier Arnold had protested
in *Culture and Anarchy* against the unwisdom and in-
justice of allowing British policy toward Ireland to be
dictated by the prejudices of the English and Scottish
middle class and against the impudence of the Liberal
chiefs in pretending at the very time when they were kow-
towing to these prejudices that they were acting in the
light of permanent principles of wisdom and justice. "A
disinterested observer," he now remarks, "will see an
action so controlled to be what it is, and will call it what
it is."[75] He returns to his claim that he speaks from the
vantage point of disinterested observation and reflection
with the remark, "I do not profess to be a politician, but
simply one of a disinterested class of observers, who with
no organised and embodied set of supporters to please, set

themselves to observe honestly and to report faithfully the state and prospects of our civilisation."[76] The impulse to write this essay came from Arnold's pleasure when a few independent spirits in the Liberal party joined the Irish members of the House in supporting the O'Conor Don's resolution "affirming the claims of Ireland to a Catholic university" and from his disappointment and vexation when the Liberal leaders and the mass of the Liberal members voted against it. As in the discourse on "Equality," Arnold collects the suffrages of other nations; elsewhere such claims as Catholic Ireland makes are conceded: the French allowed the Protestants of Alsace a special status in the University of Strasbourg; the Germans allowed the Catholics of the Rhineland a special status in the University of Bonn. The British are less just and less reasonable. Their policy is inspired by the nonsensical notion of the middle-class Nonconformists in England and Scotland for whom the Catholic religion is a dismal lie and their own a perfect expression of revealed truth. The moment the Nonconformist dragon is mentioned, Arnold's disinterested manner begins to wear thin. The Arnold of the angrier parts of *Culture and Anarchy* revives when he describes the Westminster Confession as "whatever Principal Tulloch may think . . . . a document absolutely antiquated, sterile, and worthless" and the Presbyterian church service as "perhaps the most dismal performance ever invented by man."[77] "I often wished," says Sir Leslie Stephen, "that I too had a little sweetness and light that I might be able to say such nasty things of my enemies."[78]

When Arnold returned to the Irish theme in 1881, he hit upon a device which would enable him to establish in strong terms the defects of the English middle class and yet repress his own annoyance with them. In "The In-compatibles" he remarks: "I have said so much about this class at divers times and what I have said about it has made me so many enemies that I prefer to take the words of anybody rather than myself for showing the impression which this class is likely to make, and which it does make";[79] instead of his own perceptions and judgment he offers Dickens' in *David Copperfield*. Dickens is one of their own kind, "intimately indeed did Dickens know the middle class; he was bone of its bone and flesh of its flesh."[80] And yet for Dickens its typical schoolmaster is Mr. Creakle, with his ignorance, his tyranny, and his floggings; and for Dickens its serious specimens are the Murdstones, hard, self-righteous, and unlovely; and its light-minded specimen is Mr. Quinion. Saintsbury com-plains of the extended use Arnold makes of *David Copper-field*, "a comparison not wholly improper as a mere illus-tration in passing" but "worked to death and turned in-side out and upside down, for some twenty mortal pages."[81] Saintsbury's Tory sympathies were offended by Arnold's opinions on Ireland, and it is possibly for this rea-son that he comes so far short of doing justice to the re-sourcefulness with which Arnold keeps the figures from *David Copperfield* as a fascinating living barrier between himself and his middle-class readers. It is in large part be-cause of the use of this barrier that "The Incompatibles" is among the quietest of Arnold's political and social es-says. He appears to have been conscious of the quiet tone he adopted. He closes the introductory passage by draw-ing a contrast between the conventional and pedantic dis-cussions of Irish policy which go on among political par-tisans and conversations conducted in "a *quiet* and simple way" by disinterested observers, "lovers of humane life and of civilisation," who are able to "see the matter as it really stands"; "I imagine myself," he says at a later point, "to be at present talking *quietly* to open-minded, unprejudiced, simple people, free from class spirit and party spirit, resolved . . . . to see things as they really are"; perhaps it may comfort the oppressed and misjudged Irish, the victims of Creakle and Murdstone to know that hidden beneath the crust of party politics in England "there are a number of *quiet* people" who believe that English party-politics is a gross Philistine thing, a thing which must continue for a time, but "these *quiet* people . . . . condemn and disown it; and they do their best to prepare opinion for banishing it"; to take a phrase which comes later in the essay, Arnold is trying to write from the vantage point of the "*quiet* bystander";[82] and it is in large part because of the device of using *David Copperfield* that he so admirably succeeds in retaining his position.

The year after the appearance of "The Incompatibles" in the *Nineteenth Century* the essay was reprinted as the first of the *Irish Essays and Others*. In the Preface to the collection Arnold defines the aim of his considerations of policy toward Ireland in terms which remind one of the most disinterested passages in "The Function of Criticism":

English people keep asking themselves what we ought to do about Ireland. The great contention of these essays is, that in order to attach Ireland to us solidly, English people have not only to *do* something different from what they have done hitherto, they have also to *be* something different from what they have been hitherto. As a whole, as a community, they have to acquire a larger and sweeter temper, a larger and more lucid mind. And this is indeed no light task, yet it is the capital task now appointed to us, and our safety depends on our accomplishing it: to *be* something different, much more, even, than to *do* something different.[83]

It is because of Arnold's success in "The Incompatibles" in himself being something different from the contentious and supercilious critic, prone to saying "such nasty things" about his enemies, in rising to the plane of the disinterested disposition, that this essay becomes one of the most persuasive of his writings, that it wears so exceedingly well. I should think it was of "The Incompatibles" that Mr. Carleton Stanley was chiefly mindful when, amid the troubles of 1913 in Dublin and Belfast, he recalled not the works of Mrs. J. R. Green, not even Swift's or Burke's, but the *Irish Essays* of Matthew Arnold.[84] John Morley, who was for years face to face with the Irish problem as no other Victorian man of letters ever was, speaks of Arnold's "insight into the roots of the Irish case, and the strong persistence with which he pressed that case upon unwilling ears" as "in some ways the most remarkable instance of his many-sided and penetrating vision."[85]

The quietness, the disinterestedness of the Irish essays, the preoccupation Arnold shows in them for the long future and for the lasting prescriptions of reason and justice, are representative of Arnold's political and social criticism in his last decade. Ireland was his principal theme. About purely domestic policies he did not write much until after his retirement took place in 1886.[86]

After Ireland his main subject was America. Toward the Americans he desired to be conciliatory. His first essay on the United States, "A Word about America," was written and printed before he formed his project of visiting the country;[87] it is for no accidental practical reason that Arnold is conciliatory in it; it is because he was aware of the

extreme sensitiveness of Americans, who appeared to him
to be a people without skins, so intense was their resentment and disturbance at the pricks of foreign criticism.
The strategy in "A Word about America" is elaborately
disinterested; its obtrusiveness is its one serious flaw. It
consists in a many-toned refusal to join battle. Late in the
essay the strategy reaches its height when Arnold feels he
must give instances of what he disapproves in American
civilization. He gives two; and, both in the choices and in
the juggler's agility with which he manipulates them, his
concern about the susceptibilities of Americans is extraordinary. His first example is a description by an English
traveler of life in a rural family near Denver. In selecting
for illustration the crude life of the frontier rather than the
world of the eastern seaboard "I prefer," he says, "to follow a course which would, I know, deliver me over a prey
into the Americans' hands, if I were really holding a controversy with them and attacking their civilization."[88] His
second instance is taken not from America but from Australia; it is a heavily comic report of a concert at Sydney
in which the manner is that of Mark Twain at his worst.
But, Arnold reminds the American reader, "This is not
Mark Twain, not an American humorist at all; it is the
Bathurst Sentinel."[89] There, there! he appears to say, I have
uttered my criticisms, and you must admit that they did
not hurt. He has uttered his criticisms, he has made it plain
that there are qualities in American life that he disapproves,
and he has done so with a maximum of inoffensiveness and
detachment. One's only complaint is that Arnold makes a
parade of the inoffensiveness and the detachment. This becomes actually frivolous when toward the end of the
essay Arnold writes: "And now having up to this point

neglected all the arts of the controversialist, having merely made inquiries of my American friends as to the real state of their civilization, inquiries which they are free to answer in their own favor if they like, I am going to leave the advantage with them to the end."[90] Where, we must inquire, were the arts of the controversialist, or some of them, so dexterously exercised, with such pleasure in possessing them and knowing how to use them? Where were inquiries pointed so carefully that they admitted so clearly of but one answer? What advantage can there be for the opponent unless by simplicity of mind he has taken the appearances of things for their reality? "A Word about America" is perhaps the most striking instance of all Arnold's writings of a disinterested strategy applied to the service of an interested disposition. Brownell's remark about the manner in which Arnold managed to insinuate his criticisms of America in the discourses he delivered here is no less appropriate to this essay: the Americans "found something a little superfine and superfluous in the attempt to tell [them] delicately that [they were] gross."[91]

The manner and management of the first of the *Discourses in America*, "Numbers," the only one among them in which Arnold is concerned with the political and social problems of America, are much the same as in "A Word about America"; but the inoffensiveness and detachment are less obtrusive and ring more true.[92] In his first essay on America after returning to England, "A Word More about America," almost all is praise: Arnold speaks from his observation about the excellence of American political institutions and maintains the role of a sympathetic alien. It was not until, in the last months of his life, he wrote "Civilisation in the United States" that he had again to solve the problem of insinuating criticism of American life. But of this essay I shall say what must be said in the last pages of this chapter.

V

Shortly before his retirement Arnold unfolded to Goldwin Smith[92] the use he intended to make of his leisure. He would attempt once more to compose the dramatic poem on Lucretius; and there were other poetic subjects, which he did not name, and perhaps he was not yet too old to make something of them. On political affairs he proposed to make but one more comment.[93] In fact he wrote no poetry in the two years which remained to him; and instead of one political article he wrote five.[94] The month following his retirement saw the appearance of the first in a series of four political articles in the *Nineteenth Century*. The motive which impelled Arnold to write this and the sequent articles is clearly given in the opening paragraph of the third in the series, "Up to Easter":

> For my part, as I grow old, and profit, I hope, by the lessons of experience, I think the chief good, that which above all makes life worth living, is *to be of use*. In pursuit of this good, I find myself from time to time brought, as almost every one in the present critical juncture must be brought, to politics. I know the objections to meddling with them; I know and can perfectly understand the impatience and irritation which my intervention in these matters causes to many people. Nothing I should like better than to feel assured that I should never have occasion to write on politics again. I write on other subjects with much more pleasure.[95]

"The present critical juncture!" Again a conviction of crisis is sufficient to sweep Arnold off his course; once more the desire to be of immediate use is all-powerful with him. Perhaps the present shift is more significant than any of those that preceded; for when he turned from the pursuit of letters to write *Culture and Anarchy* and again to write *Literature and Dogma*, he might reasonably have hoped to have many years before him. But in the spring of 1885 he began to have alarming pains across his chest; and remembering the death of his father and of his father before him from sudden cardiac weakness, Arnold must have seen the future as unmistakably brief. The pains grew in intensity, and they remained for longer periods; and when he was in America in the summer of 1886 he had fears that he might not live to return to England.[96] What he did not write at once it was probable that he would never write, and yet he wrote of the immediate political issues of the time.

The political articles of Arnold's last two years have not been collected; they do not appear even in the fifteen-volume edition of his works. Nor is this a matter for regret. They are as nearly ephemeral as anything Arnold wrote could be; that is to say, although they are informed by his lasting principles and expressed in the beautiful quiet idiom of his latter years, they are saturated with the immediate political issues of the late eighties and above all with the luckless proposals and enactments for Ireland of the Liberal and Conservative parties. If they were generally available, we should have a far truer conception of the final state of Arnold's mind. For readers in our time he ended by writing of Tolstoi and Milton and Shelley; but in fact he ended by writing much more about Mr. Gladstone. If we are to understand the tone of the essay on Shelley, it is necessary to come to it from the political journalism which preceded and followed it.

"What a move is this of Gladstone's in the Irish matter!

and what apprehensions it gives me!"[97] Arnold wrote to his sister at the end of 1885, shortly after the Liberal triumph in the general elections of the late autumn and the prime minister's statement of policy on Irish Home Rule. What followed the exclamation is excised, but its general tendency may be construed from the fashion in which Arnold spoke of Gladstone in a letter of the following month to Goldwin Smith, which comes to us free of the censorship of the Arnold family or of that faithful admirer of Gladstone, George Russell. To Goldwin Smith, Arnold wrote fresh from the excitement of a mission to imperial Germany in which he had met Bismarck: Bismarck, he owns, "speaks badly, but one contrasts his powerful character with the fertile tongue of one adored William, not to our advantage. With our William everything is possible; still his Home Rule plans I cannot believe in till he produces them. As now attributed to him, they have every conceivable vice which a plan for Ireland can have."[98] The comparison of Gladstone with Bismarck is carried on at great length, if a little less pungently, in one of the articles for the *Nineteenth Century*.[99] The distaste, the contempt, for Gladstone which Arnold had for so long restrained or muffled in ironical epithets and phrases poured out more than once in these late political articles. What passes for Gladstonian statesmanship is no more, Arnold claims, than acute perception of the essential desires of his supporters—the English and Scottish middle-class Philistine Dissenters—combined with skill in manipulating these desires in speeches and in translating them into the law of the land. The verdict on Gladstone is that he is no more than an eloquent manager. When in the elections of 1886 Gladstone was driven out of office, essentially because of his Irish policy, and a Conservative majority of massive size was returned, Arnold was for the time being tranquilized. It was not that he counted on wisdom in the policies of a Conservative administration toward Ireland—that was an error he never made and was incapable of making; he counted merely on caution and inaction as warrant that there would be no rushing into an irremediable mistake. He knew that a bold and imaginative policy was necessary and that it was unthinkable in a Conservative administration; he knew that delay or recession was dangerous; but it was less dangerous than Mr. Gladstone in Downing Street, with his peculiar brand of boldness and imagination. As 1887 passed and the early months of 1888, Arnold's tranquillity was shaken; he recognized how unsatisfactory was the Conservative policy toward Ireland and how perilous was delay. No other temporal problem weighed upon him so heavily in the last months of his life.

The essay on Shelley, which appeared less than four months before he died, was the last of Arnold's major literary studies. He turned to it from writing about politics, and to writing about politics he returned. The occasion was Edward Dowden's biography of the poet, and it is astonishing to note the political twist that Arnold gives to a comment upon Dowden's somewhat turgid style: "Is it that the Home Rulers have so loaded the language that even an Irishman who is not one of them catches something of their full habit of style?"[100] The saturation with Irish politics is even more remarkable when, having occasion to refer to a servant of Shelley's, Arnold salutes him as "bearing the prophetic name of Healy."[101] But the political virus enters far more deeply into the essay. It is very unlike the rest of Arnold's late literary essays; it does not offer any valuable discriminations, nor does it exalt the qualities which nourish the disposition of disinterestedness.

Dowden, Arnold complains, "holds a brief for Shelley; he pleads for Shelley as an advocate pleads for his client." The strain of pleading, Arnold says, will beget "in many readers of the story which Professor Dowden has to tell, impatience and revolt." Unquestionably these were the attitudes it determined in one reader: the note which sounds throughout the greater part of Arnold's essay is that of the prosecutor. "I propose," he warns the reader, "to mark firmly what is ridiculous and odious in the Shelley brought to our knowledge by the new materials."[102] On the circle in which Shelley lived and wrote, Arnold's judgment is "What a set! what a world!"[103] Now one's judgment of Shelley's circle, whether in terms of ethics or of taste, may well be a severe one if it is brought in contrast with, let us say, Wordsworth's circle; but the contrasting circle which Arnold's judgment introduces is astonishing by its irrelevance. Arnold speaks of the Oxford of Copleston, Keble, and Hawkins, and he might have added his own father's name, "the clerical and respectable Oxford of those old times." When did any poetic group in England or out of it live and feel in the fashion of intellectual middle-aged clergy of the Church of England? In a letter written in 1840 to another middle-aged intellectual clergyman, William Charles Lake, later dean of Durham, Thomas Arnold shows how far he was from understanding the processes of a young poet. He complains:

Matt does not know what it is to work because he so little knows what it is to think. But I am hopeful about him more than I was; his amiableness of temper seems very great, and some of his faults appear to me less; and he is so loving to me that it ought to make me not only hopeful, but very patient and long-suffering towards him. Besides I think that he is not so idle as he was, and that there is a better prospect of his beginning to read in earnest. Alas! that we should have to talk of prospect only, and of no performance as yet which deserves the name of earnest reading.

Lord Coleridge, writing from the most intimate knowledge, has told how imperfect was Thomas Arnold's appreciation of the young poet in his household;[104] and it is difficult to believe that either Hawkins or Copleston would have received in a more generous fashion a spirit to whom poetry was more than piety. The contrast that Arnold sets up is one possible only to an exasperated mind. It is true that Arnold intended, after he had firmly marked Shelley's misdeeds—and soundly flogged him for them—to assure us that our "former beautiful and lovable Shelley nevertheless survives." But his heart was not in the second part of the undertaking; he allowed himself but a few pages for it;[105] he applied himself to the demonstration of the survival of the former Shelley without a trace of enthusiasm; and he allowed the poetry of Shelley to be crowded out of the essay entirely.[106]

The judgment that he has offered is that of a crusty conservative; it is biased, harsh, and supercilious. It comes from an Arnold made angry and alarmed by the exploits of Mr. Gladstone, not from the Arnold who only a few years before had written with such a vibrant generosity of Byron. Once again, as so often, he did not accomplish what he set out to do; he even meditated an essay in which he would examine the poetry of Shelley and set the balance right.[107] He did not live to write it.

The last of the social essays, "Civilisation in the United States," published in the month of Arnold's death, does not bear so obvious a mark of the author's alarm. It is an essay in discriminations and is conducted as the report of an equable, if not wholly disinterested, observer and judge.

MATTHEW ARNOLD

Arnold begins by establishing his fundamental sympathies with America, with its political system truly consonant with the modern world as the British is not, with its social principles and practices based, as the British are not, on a living conviction of the equality of men. The political and social problems, he insists, are on the whole adequately solved in America, inadequately in Great Britain. Before he ventures his most severe comments on the American failure to solve the great remaining problem, the problem of achieving civilization, he reminds his readers how severe his comments have been, and how often repeated, on the British failure to solve this problem. The structure of the essay is admirable as a piece of persuasion, as fine as the best of the Irish essays. But in the details the advantages Arnold has won by the general structure are sacrificed. Irritated by the complacence of Americans, he diagnoses the nation as afflicted by "morbid nervousness"; he denies "distinction" to Abraham Lincoln; he quotes with unqualified approval the phrase of a French critic, "la dure inintelligence des Américains du Nord."[108] The tone is supercilious, and at times the rhythm is even petulant. Besides, if the introduction of Arnold's own resentment against American newspapers adds zest to the essay, it nevertheless distorts a substantial part of it to read like a personal protest. The effect becomes—what Arnold would have deplored if he had recognized its existence—personal and complaining. It is true that the Irish crisis is not mentioned—and in view of the Irish-Americans it might easily have been—but the strain on Arnold's nerves that it brought about has had its way with many a paragraph in the essay. Arnold's criticism ends as it had so often developed, in an inconsistency of manner, an uncertainty of touch.

CHAPTER SEVEN

Terminal Note: The Way of Disinterestedness and the Way of Practical Criticism

T HE oscillation between the poles of detachment and action, of artistic contemplation and practical criticism, in which so much of Matthew Arnold's life was passed, makes him a figure of special significance for our time as for his own. His mind and self formed the theater for a struggle between two great groups of forces which have worked with so much effect on so many artists from his age to ours as to have become a momentous fact in modern culture. There is the group of forces which bid an artist become wholly a participant in the activity of his time and place, speaking to his age and acting on it with a didactic simplicity of motive; and there is the group of forces which bid him move steadily and disinterestedly along the internal line of his art.

The impulse to address his own age and to operate on it is wholly legitimate in the artist. But the artist relates himself most successfully to his age when he remains within the terms of his art, the terms within which his special power is effective. It is quite possible that a mind of another sort, a political theorist's or a general commentator's, may affect the age more profoundly than the mind of the artist can do. It appears to many that at the present moment this is so. But the artist is not a political theorist or a general commentator, and there is no real choice for him between the terms of art and the terms of political theory and general comment. If he essays political theory or general comment, he is abandoning his right hand for his left: he competes at conspicuous disadvantage with a host of minds adept and trained for the role he haltingly attempts.

Remaining within the terms of art, his address will be effective. The case of Browning is an example of extreme effectiveness.

The Browning of *Men and Women* is a triumphant example of faithfully artistic communication with his contemporaries and appropriate action upon them. There is scarcely a notable long poem in that collection which does not flash a light upon a major Victorian issue: The idealism of the Pre-Raphaelites as opposed to the modes and spirit of artistic realism? The comment is to be made out from "Fra Lippo Lippi." The role of art in the social order? It is all in "How It Strikes a Contemporary," although Browning appears to speak only of a nameless Spanish writer and a nameless Spanish king of long ago. Science and faith? "An Epistle Containing the Strange Medical Experience of Karshish, an Arab Physician." And when in "Caliban upon Setebos; or Natural Theology in the Island," Browning so admirably brings before us Prospero's magic isle, he would not have the alert reader's imagination and speculation rest there but would invite them to pass to another island in another age where there was a fierce hubbub about natural theology. Of the social and economic issues in the Victorian age it is true that Browning's poetry says nothing profound; but on them his deeper thoughts never ran. With this exception, he touches luminously on everything that the great quarterlies and weeklies kept under debate; but, unlike the artists who deviated into practical criticism, he was faithful to the methods of his art and wrote in constant realization of the impulses of his truly creative self. In his old age, it is true, his art declined, and most of his magic was withdrawn from him; but the decline came no earlier than his sixtieth year, when the art of most poets has begun to weaken. He would at any time have fully understood Tennyson's message to Arnold, so similar to Turgenev's letter to Tolstoi: "Tell Mat not to write any more of those prose things like *Literature and Dogma*, but to give us something like his 'Thyrsis,' 'Scholar Gipsy,' or 'Forsaken Merman.' "

Matthew Arnold is a particularly complicated instance of the conflict between disinterestedness and action, art and practical criticism. In him the struggle begins early; it rises in an uneven intensity, creating crises large and small the entire length of his career; there are moments in which it abates astonishingly and moments in which it is wholly suspended, with happy result; and the conflict is unsettled at the very end. If Arnold had outlived the acute phase of the Irish crisis which began in 1885, he might have added another collection or two of literary and social essays wise and temperate and even perhaps an admirable elegy, on the death, suppose, of Cardinal Newman—the most suggestive theme for an elegy that the century might have offered him. Arnold's work in the Education Department was a notable complicating factor. He did not become interested in the large issues that his daily work presented until he was almost forty; he then began to put forward extremely specific proposals for the reform first of elementary and then of secondary education. But when Arnold became a practical critic of education, he was not at all in the role of Ruskin speaking of political economy—he spoke as an expert. "Over all those Victorian years," says Mr. G. M. Young, "hovers the airy and graceful spirit of the School Inspector, ingeminating *Porro unum est necessarium*—Organize your secondary education." The airy and graceful spirit not of the author of "The Scholar Gipsy" and the "Stanzas from the Grande Chartreuse" but of the official in the Education Department. The poet and the inspector might, perhaps, have pursued careers as separate as Housman's in textual criticism and lyric poetry. But I have shown how Arnold was led on from educational criticism to a general criticism of politics and society; from proposals concerning the part of the social structure which he knew as an expert to the rest of the structure concerning which he knew scarcely more than Ruskin himself. He did not allow for the vast difference between his accurate and always accumulating knowledge about education and his vague notions about, let us say, the history of the English middle class or of the Church of England. Arnold was never a learned man; and he did not have the learned man's methods of inquiry or his scruples about judging in areas where his knowledge was scanty. So he passed lightheartedly from the practical criticism of the expert to the practical criticism of the artist wandering beyond his true scope.

In his poetry and in his literary criticism and indeed in not a few social essays, he succeeds in communicating with his contemporaries on issues that are comparable in importance with those which Browning illuminated, remaining as Browning did within the terms of art. His case becomes yet more interesting as we recognize him capable of extraordinary success and extraordinary failure within the bounds of a single work, often a poem or a brief essay. The style which for a space has been beautifully even and accomplished will suddenly break into pieces; the impeccable manner sustained long enough to have seemed second nature will suddenly exhibit some gross and incredible flaw; or the structure will be perfectly disinterested and some detail will crop up drenched in controversial or petulant personal feeling. Such incoherences, artistic disasters, indicative of a divided mind and spirit, may occur in any of the genres that Arnold practiced and in any period of his career, although—as might be expected from what has been observed in other writers—they are more frequent in the later years.

Excursions into practical criticism are always creditable to the artist as citizen: they do honor to the heart and the conscience. The artist is not the whole of the man; and it is to be expected of a mature man that he will participate in the political activities of the state, not only carrying out explicit political obligations but on due occasion associating himself in such activities as protesting particular injustices and working for justice. But such activities are undertaken not by the artist but by other parts of a man's nature. It is a very different outcome of political interest when for political purposes the man uses his own peculiar instrument, when he turns his art to the service of practical criticism. There is, unfortunately, no ground whatever for the supposition that in his political activities the man who is an artist will be unusually wise; he is, indeed, more likely to be the "unpractical half-cracked artist or author" of Morris' bitter phrase; and there are few spectacles more depressing than that of a great artist making a fool of himself with the instrument which he has used in his art, because he is inflamed with some political (or, to be sure, religious or any other extra-artistic) purpose. The Victorian age witnessed such a spectacle in the 1860's.

When in the autumn of 1865 an outbreak of the colored population occurred in one Jamaican county, Governor Eyre proclaimed martial law and allowed it to continue in effect long after the situation was in hand. A fearful vengeance was exacted in the flogging and execution of men and women, preceded by no careful inquiries as to the role individuals had played in the outbreak. Among the victims was George William Gordon, a leading Jamaican of mixed blood, who appears on the evidence not only of his conduct in the fatal year but of his whole career to have been an estimable and perhaps even an admirable character. A Royal Commission was named; and by it the conduct of the governor was strongly censured. It was not censured by Thomas Carlyle. Carlyle put himself at the head of a committee to aid Eyre and drafted a petition which was to be submitted to the House of Commons. Carlyle praised Eyre's headlong and vehement behavior as "courageous prompt and skilful conduct . . . . which seems to us to be of heroic quality rather, and were of supreme indispensability in the position where he was." Gordon he describes as "proved in an English Court of Justice . . . . a man whom it was the duty of all British subjects to assist in getting executed, by the nearest and highest gallows there was a road to." On Eyre's conduct the judgment of the earl of Carnarvon, speaking for the government, was somewhat different: "Promptitude, courage, fearlessness of responsibility, if not accompanied by a sound judgment on the part of the person who possesses them, become faults rather than virtues and are in the nature of a curse rather than a blessing to the Colony with the Government of which that person is entrusted." Nor did Lord Carnarvon agree with Carlyle in the great seer, biographer, and historian's estimate of the character of George William Gordon. He continued: "Much has been said respecting the case of Mr. Gordon. I do not wish to say anything about it, and for this reason—It is a most terrible case and one that is indefensible." In drafting the petition some would say that Carlyle, even if he drew upon the chief resources of his general literary manner, was acting not in the quality of an artist but as a simple citizen. The defense would be a specious one; but it need not concern us, since Carlyle was not willing to let his advocacy of Eyre rest with the petition and the political activities which followed. He dragged the Eyre case into a prominent part of his next—and last—important essay, "Shooting Niagara—and After," published in 1867. As he considered the awful perspective of a democratic regime opened by the Reform Bill of the previous year, England's ingratitude to Eyre seemed to him a portent of what Carlylean heroes would experience. Now for the last time speaking to England with his full vigor of mind and manner, he attacked a government which, "instead of rewarding their Governor Eyre, throw him out of window to a small loud group, small as now appears, and nothing but a group or knot of rabid Nigger-Philanthropists, barking furiously in the gutter." Among the gutter-barkers were John Stuart Mill and Thomas Henry Huxley. This is the outcome of a victory for practical criticism over art, art which in this very discourse is described as "very fine and ornamental, but only to persons sitting at their ease; to persons still wrestling with deadly chaos, and still fighting for dubious existence.... a mockery rather." The folly and wickedness of Carlyle's practical criticism, not content with havoc worked in that area, have forced their way into the artistic work, which he despised or affected to despise and ruined it as well.

Nowhere in Arnold is there a statement comparable with Carlyle's pronouncements on Governor Eyre. But there are passages in Arnold's social prose in which the practical critic falls as short of reasonableness as any of the Victorian statesmen whom he so often rebuked. There is, for example, the suggestion—prudently suppressed in the third text of the work—that the proper remedy for riots is the old Roman rigor, the leaders to be hurled from the Tarpeian Rock and the rest whipped. We do not know what opinion Arnold held of Governor Eyre, but Eyre would have liked that passage in *Culture and Anarchy*. It is not to be compared with the rages of Carlyle's later years, but it points to the same dire defect; and so do many other passages, not only in the social but in the religious prose. They are the utterances of a man speaking without the privileged insight which is the artist's when he is truly and fully an artist; speaking without a notion that for the moment he has forfeited that insight; speaking also without the sobriety of judgment, long and carefully exercised by one fully informed of the range of subject under his view, by which in the controversy over Eyre the apparently quite ordinary intelligence of a minister such as Lord Carnarvon was led right, where all the genius of Carlyle was led into appalling error.

NOTES

CHAPTER I

1. William Caldwell Roscoe, *Prospective Review*, X (February, 1854), 109.

2. William Caldwell Roscoe, *National Review*, VI (April, 1858), 270.

3. *Prospective Review, op. cit.*, p. 110.

4. *Fraser's Magazine*, XLIX (February, 1854), 147.

5. Clough's paper appeared in the *North American Review* for July, 1853, and is conveniently accessible in *Prose Remains of Arthur Hugh Clough*, edited by his wife (London, 1888), pp. 355–78. The passage cited is on pp. 366–67.

6. C. B. Tinker and H. F. Lowry, *The Poetry of Matthew Arnold: A Commentary* (London, 1940), pp. 122–24.

7. *Blackwood's*, LXXV (March, 1854), 312.

8. *Prospective Review, op. cit.; Leader*, IV (December 3, 1853), 1171; *Blackwood's, loc. cit.*

9. *Fraser's Magazine, loc. cit.; Athenaeum*, No. 2183 (August 28, 1869), p. 271.

10. *Blackwood's*, LXVI (September, 1849), 343.

11. Richard Holt Hutton, "The Poetry of Matthew Arnold," collected in his *Literary Essays*. The passage cited occurs on pp. 343–44 of the 3d ed., revised and enlarged (London, 1888).

12. Henry Buxton Forman, *Our Living Poets* (London, 1871), pp. 324–29.

13. H. W. Garrod, *Poetry and the Criticism of Life* (Cambridge, Mass., 1931), pp. 49–50.

14. Carleton Stanley, *Matthew Arnold* (Toronto, 1938), p. 41.

15. Stuart Sherman, *Matthew Arnold: How To Know Him* (Indianapolis, 1917, 1944), pp. 76–77. (Used by special permission of the publishers, Bobbs Merrill Co.)

16. E.g., Herbert W. Paul, *Matthew Arnold* (New York, 1903), pp. 47–48; George Saintsbury, *Matthew Arnold* (New York, 1899), pp. 42–43; Tinker and Lowry, *op. cit.*, pp. 212–14.

17. In my "The Scholar Gipsy: An Interpretation," *Revue anglo-américaine*, XII (February, 1935), 224–25.

18. The Preface is conveniently accessible in *The Poems of Matthew Arnold, 1840–1867*, ed. Sir Arthur Quiller-Couch (London, 1942) (cited hereafter as "*Poems*"), pp. 1–16. The passage cited is on p. 8.

19. *Dublin University Magazine*, LI (March, 1858), 337. The passage comes from "Resignation" (*Poems*, p. 91, ll. 225–26).

20. *Athenaeum*, No. 2079 (August 31, 1867), p. 266; *Victoria Magazine*, XI (August, 1868), 382. The passage is representative of the short poem "Pis-aller" (*Poems*, p. 413, ll. 9–10).

21. Tinker and Lowry, *op. cit.*, p. 24.

22. Lionel Johnson, *Post liminium* (London, 1911), p. 293. The line is "Parting" (*Poems*, p. 133), l. 53; Johnson omits the hyphen.

23. "To the Duke of Wellington" (*Poems*, p. 59, ll. 3–6).

24. Garrod, *op. cit.*, p. 54. The passage is in the second part of "Balder Dead" (*Poems*, pp. 248–49, ll. 91–99).

25. Saintsbury, *op. cit.*, pp. 38–39.

26. Tinker and Lowry, *op. cit.*, pp. 37–41; there is an interesting reference to Arnold's late opinion of the second part of the poem in a letter to F. T. Palgrave, cited by G. W. E. Russell, *Matthew Arnold* (New York, 1904), p. 42. The letter shows how uncertain was Arnold as to the value of many of his poems.

27. *Essays in Criticism, Second Series* (1st ed.; London, 1888), pp. 135–36, 163–72.

28. *Ibid.*, pp. 135–36.

29. *Ibid.*, pp. 166, 170.

30. *Ibid.*, p. 49.

31. A. C. Bradley, *A Miscellany* (London, 1929), p. 142 ("Shelley and Arnold's Critique of His Poetry").

32. "Epilogue to Lessing's Laocoön" (*Poems*, p. 413, ll. 1–3).

33. T. S. Eliot, *The Use of Poetry and the Use of Criticism* (Cambridge, Mass., 1933), p. 104, n. 1.

34. Lewis Gates, *Selections from the Prose Writings of Matthew Arnold* (New York, 1897), pp. lix–lxxvi.

35. *Essays in Criticism, Second Series*, pp. 196, 197.

36. The introduction to the *Six Selected Lives from Johnson's Lives of the English Poets* (London, 1878) unaccountably fails to offer a portrait of the critic or an analysis of his method in criticism. In theme it is comparable with such an essay as "The Literary Influence of Academies," and there is no foothold for emotion.

37. *Mixed Essays* (London, 1879), pp. 238, 239.

38. *Ibid.*, p. 242. The passage quoted is from the final paragraph of the essay on Milton; two phrases have been omitted.

39. This is the first line of Shelley's "Sonnet; England in 1819" (*Complete Poetical Works of Shelley*, ed. T. Hutchinson [Oxford, 1904], p. 637).

40. Gates, *op. cit.*, pp. lix–lx.

41. Garrod, *op. cit.*, p. 83.

42. *British Quarterly Review*, XLIII (October, 1865), 250. For Arnold's satisfaction with the review see *Letters of Matthew Arnold*, ed. G.W. E. Russell (New York, 1895), I, 310: "I have been struck with the much

greater caring for my poems and knowledge of them than I had any notion of. This is what is chiefly remarkable in the *British Quarterly* article."

43. W. J. Courthope, *Life in Poetry, Law in Taste* (London, 1901), pp. 137–38.

44. *Literature and Dogma* (1st ed.; London, 1873), p. 306.

45. *Literature and Dogma* (popular ed.; London, 1883), pp. vi–vii.

46. *Culture and Anarchy*, ed. J. Dover Wilson (Cambridge, 1935), p. 84. This is a reprint of the first edition in book form.

47. Garrod, *op. cit.*, p. 83.

48. Walter Pater, *Miscellaneous Studies* (London, 1895), p. 17.

49. *Times* ("University Intelligence"), October 26, 1864.

50. Sherman, *op. cit.*, p. 135; W. C. Brownell, *Victorian Prose Masters* (New York, 1915), p. 159; Lionel Trilling, *Matthew Arnold* (New York, 1939), p. 203; Paul, *op. cit.*, p. 77; Saintsbury, *op. cit.*, p. 85.

51. Geoffrey Tillotson, "Matthew Arnold: The Critic and the Advocate," in *Essays by Divers Hands*, ed. Gordon Bottomley, XX (new ser.; London, 1943), 29–41.

52. At the close of the essay Arnold points out its character as introduction to the volume *Essays in Criticism* [First Series] (1st ed.; London, 1865), p. 40.

53. *Ibid.*, p. 18.

54. Tillotson, *op. cit.*, p. 31.

55. *Essays in Criticism* [First Series], p. 26.

56. *Ibid.*, pp. 25, 27.

57. Thomas Hardy, *A Pair of Blue Eyes*, chaps. xxxviii, xxxix. It is interesting to note in an earlier chapter (iv) the phrase "the neutral tone of disinterested criticism." The term "disinterested" is not rare in the writing of the time, however; it occurs frequently in Dickens, Thackeray, and Meredith.

CHAPTER II

1. C. B. Tinker and H. F. Lowry, *The Poetry of Matthew Arnold: A Commentary* (London, 1940), p. 322.

2. "Cromwell" (*The Poems of Matthew Arnold, 1840–1867*, ed. Sir Arthur Quiller-Couch [London, 1942] [cited hereafter as *"Poems"*], p. 30, ll. 101–2).

3. *Ibid.*, p. 58.

4. Tinker and Lowry, *op. cit.*, p. 25.

5. *Poems*, p. 36. This poem was originally entitled simply "Sonnet," subsequently "Quiet Work." Tinker and Lowry remark: "In his final arrangement Arnold restored it to its position as the first poem in the book, a distinction which it received in all later editions. It is clear that the poet regarded it as of primary importance with respect to his poetry and to his philosophy of life" (*ibid.*, p. 22). I trust that the argument I am setting forth will tend to confirm this opinion by showing the central importance of the poem in the early formulation of the ideal of the distinterested disposition.

The fluctuations in Arnold's conception of nature are admirably analyzed in Professor Joseph Warren Beach's *The Concept of Nature in Nineteenth Century English Poetry* (New York, 1936), pp. 397-405.

6. The relevant passages are these:

"Into the silence of the groves and woods
 I will go forth"

"Mycerinus" (*Poems*, p. 38, ll. 67-68)

"The cheerful silence of the fells."
                    "Resignation" (*ibid.*, p. 88, l. 67)

"Yet, Fausta, the mute turf we tread"
                    "Resignation" (*ibid.*, p. 92, l. 263)

"Ere the long night, whose stillness brooks no star,"
                    "To a Gipsy Child" (*ibid.*, p. 78, l. 45)

"As the kindling glances,
 Queen-like and clear,
 Which the bright moon lances
 From her tranquil sphere"
                    "The Voice" (*ibid.*, p. 73, ll. 1-4)

In each case there is contrast between the silence of nature and the character of human life: Mycerinus and his revelers profane the silence of the groves and woods with their fevered revelry; the poet in "Resignation" has an unquiet and volatile spirit; the long silent night in "To a Gipsy Child" is in contrast with the rush of life; the silence of the moon in "The Voice" is in contrast with the turmoil of the heart.

7. "The World and the Quietist" (*Poems*, p. 84) is an imaginary dialogue with a friend who contends that Arnold's devotion to calm is out of date in a time when will and activity are the primary values approved by the world and sanctioned by the movement of society. "In utrumque paratus," which is paired with it, presents two conceptions of the universe, one of them attributing its origin to the "silent mind of one all pure," the other attributing its origin to a wild whirling of the groaning earth.

8. "Resignation" is packed with passages bearing upon the theme. Those to which the words quoted belong are:

"To whom each moment in its race,
 Crowd as we will its neutral space,
 Is but a quiet watershed"

ll. 255-57

"And though Fate grudge to thee and me
 The Poet's rapt security"

ll. 243-44

"Yet they, believe me, who await
 No gifts from Chance, have conquer'd Fate.
 They, winning room to see and hear,

And to men's business not too near,
Through clouds of individual strife
Draw homewards to the general Life"

ll. 245-50

9. The themes are notably developed in most of the sonnets, in the "Fragment of an Antigone," and in the exquisite close of "The Forsaken Merman."

10. The close of the sonnet is a striking piece of unreserved eulogy. Arnold hails the duke as "Thou" who

"hast become
Laborious, persevering, serious, firm"
and whose track, therefore,

"across the fretful foam
Of vehement actions without scope or term,
Call'd History, keeps a splendour: due to wit,
Which saw *one* clue to life, and follow'd it"

Poems, p. 59

11. The most significant lines are:
"The Poet, to whose mighty heart
Heaven doth a quicker pulse impart,
Subdues that energy to scan
Not his own course, but that of Man"

ll. 144-47

The passage down to l. 198 is an elaboration of the participation which is much more intimate than the word "scan" suggests (*Poems*, pp. 90-91).

12. The portrait culminates:
"such a price
The Gods exact for song;
To become what we sing"

Poems, p. 47, ll. 232-34

13. "To a Friend" in *Poems*, p. 40, ll. 8-14.

14. "Stanzas in Memory of the Author of *Obermann*" was later called simply "Obermann." The portraits of Goethe and Wordsworth (ll. 49-68) should be compared with those in "Memorial Verses," written in 1850 on the occasion of Wordsworth's death (*Poems*, pp. 162-64). The lines quoted from the "Stanzas" come immediately after the portraits of Goethe and Wordsworth.

15. "Stanzas," ll. 101-4.

16. *Essays in Criticism* [First Series] (1st ed.: London, 1865), p. 24.

17. Arnold recommends oriental wisdom to Clough in letters of March 1, 4, and 8, 1848; the passage quoted is from the letter of March 4 (see *Letters of Matthew Arnold to Arthur Hugh Clough*, ed. H. F. Lowry [London, 1932], pp. 68-75).

18. Unfortunately, the letters from Clough to Arnold have not (with one exception irrelevant to this chapter) been discovered. The letters in which Arnold replies to Clough's lamentations and protests are those of

February 12, March 21, and May 1, 1853 (*Letters of M. A. to A. H. C.*, pp. 128–37). The positions Arnold takes in these are illuminating for the reader of almost any of the earlier letters, in which he had been less ready to generalize.

19. *Letters of M. A. to A. H. C.*, p. 129.

20. *Unpublished Letters of Matthew Arnold*, ed. Arnold Whitridge (New Haven, Conn., 1923), p. 18. Whitridge assigns 1853 as a conjectural date. The only evidences for date are (1) a reference to the behavior of the French in Italy and (2) a reference to a review of Arnold's poems in the *Spectator*. Each of his volumes was reviewed in that periodical. The reference to the French in Italy would seem more appropriate to 1849. There is an illuminating passage on Arnold's motives for withdrawal in Mr. Lionel Trilling's *Matthew Arnold* (New York, 1939), pp. 22–30.

21. *Letters of M. A. to A. H. C.*, p. 129.

22. *Unpublished Letters*, p. 32. I would suggest that a word occurring earlier in the same paragraph was either improperly written or improperly transcribed. Arnold is made to speak of the "absurdity and disadvantage of our *heredity* connexion in the minds of all people with education." He may have written this, but he cannot have meant to do so. One should read either "heredit'y"—he occasionally uses abridged forms—or "hereditary," the end of the word either slurred in haste or miswritten.

23. *Letters of M. A. to A. H. C.*, p. 122. The date is June 7, 1852.

24. *Letters of Matthew Arnold*, ed. G. W. E. Russell (New York, 1895), I, 15–16. The date is January, 1851.

25. *Letters of M. A. to A. H. C.*, p. 75.

26. *Letters*, ed. Russell, I, 3–4.

27. "Stanzas in Memory of the Author of *Obermann*" (*Poems*, p. 177, ll. 101–2).

28. The Preface is reprinted in the edition of the *Poems* to which all previous references have been made, pp. 1–16. The phrases quoted in this paragraph occur on pp. 1, 13.

29. All the material concerning Arnold's relations with Coleridge, including the letters, is drawn from E. H. Coleridge, *The Life and Correspondence of John Duke Coleridge, Lord Chief Justice of England* (London, 1904). The letter quoted has the date July 28 [1844]. A closing phrase confirms the impression of the passages quoted in the text: "I have not written as I could have wished, but the reproaches of your letter marred the frankness of mine" (I, 145–46).

30. *Ibid.*, pp. 126, 129.

31. *Letters of M. A. to A. H. C.*, pp. 55–57. Note also the astonishing close of the following letter, p. 58.

32. Mrs. Humphry Ward, *A Writer's Recollections* (New York, 1918), I, 58–60. Mrs. Ward assigns 1849 as the date of the letters quoted. See also J. A. Froude's comment in *Letters of M. A. to A. H. C.*, p. 127, n. 3.

33. Coleridge, *op. cit.*, I, 123. Arnold speaks of a volume of sermons by some cleric who differed from J. H. Newman and continues: "I neither

expect nor desire that they should change your admiration for Newman. I should be very unwilling to think they did so in my own case, but owing to my utter want of prejudice (you remember your slander) I find it perfectly possible to admire them both" (the date is January 8, 1843).

34. *Letters of M. A. to A. H. C.*, p. 61.

35. *Ibid.*, p. 63.

36. *Ibid.*, pp. 64-65.

37. *Ibid.*, pp. 98-99.

38. "To a Friend" (*Poems*, p. 40). The tribute to Homer in this sonnet is considered in chap. iii.

39. *Letters of M. A. to A. H. C.*, pp. 98-99.

40. *On the Study of Celtic Literature* (1st ed.; London, 1867), p. 148. His views on hymnology are developed here at considerable length: "Our German kinsmen and we are the great people for hymns. The Germans are very proud of their hymns, and we are very proud of ours; but it is hard to say which of the two, the German hymn-book or ours, has least poetical worth in itself, or does least to prove genuine poetical power in the people producing it. . . . . Only the German race, with its want of quick instinctive tact, of delicate sure perception, could have invented the hymn as the Germans and we have it." Arnold goes on to say that the pleasure and consolation drawn from hymns is conveyed to us not through what is the highest faculty of an Indo-European people, the "imaginative reason," but through one which is much less developed and distinguished, the "religious sentiment." Arnold returned to the subject to speak with greater sharpness in the last of the *Last Essays on Church and Religion* (London, 1877), "A Last Word on the Burials Bill": "Hymns, such as we know them, are a sort of composition which I do not at all admire. . . . . I regret their prevalence and popularity amongst us. . . . . It is bad for people to hear such words and such a tune as the words or tune of *O happy place! when shall I be, my God, with thee, to see thy face?*—worse for them to take pleasure in it. And the time will come, I hope, when we shall feel the unsatisfactoriness of our present hymns, and they will disappear from our religious services" (1st ed., p. 158). Both passages I have quoted appear in Arnold's own selection from his prose, *Passages from the Prose Writings of Matthew Arnold* ([London, 1880], pp. 48-50).

41. For comment upon this link see among others H. W. Garrod, *Poetry and the Criticism of Life* (Cambridge, Mass., 1931), pp. 35-36.

42. *Letters of M. A. to A. H. C.*, pp. 123-25.

43. The strongest evidence for these assertions about "Balder Dead," "Tristram and Iseult," and "Sohrab and Rustum" comes from the general tendency of Arnold's thought and feeling. The assertion about the relation of Balder to his world receives important confirmation from a comparison of the kinds of statements made concerning this relation and those made in Arnold's lyrics (e.g., the "Stanzas from the Grande Chartreuse") concerning the poet's own relation to his world. In the chapter dealing with *Essays in Criticism* [First Series] I have considered the likenesses between Balder

and historical persons whom Arnold profoundly admired and with whom he felt an intimate sympathy, particularly the likeness with Joseph Joubert. The close of the essay on Joubert is a suggestive passage (*Essays in Criticism* [First Series] [London, 1865], p. 252). The personal element in "Tristram and Iseult" has been considered with great suggestiveness and wisdom by Garrod (*op. cit.*, pp. 34–45). The assertion about "Sohrab and Rustum" is a pure hypothesis for which no external evidence exists. We have no adequate conception of the relation between Matthew Arnold and his father during the lifetime of Thomas Arnold; but, on the one hand, the significant likenesses between the two are touched on by every student of Matthew Arnold's character and thought; and, on the other, certain traits of dandyism, insouciance, and dashing worldliness in the young Matthew Arnold suggest a reaction away from the ethical values exemplified and inculcated by his father (see chap. vi, n. 104, for John Duke Coleridge's pregnant comment on Thomas Arnold's deficient sympathy with his son and see Thomas Arnold's letter to W. C. Lake, quoted on p. 176).

44. "Memorial Verses," ll. 29–34 (*Poems*, p. 163).

45. See W. Y. Sellar, *Roman Poets of the Augustan Age: Virgil* (Oxford, 1883): "It is evident that Virgil thought of Lucretius as the poet who had held up the one ideal to the imagination and the severer mood of his countrymen, and of himself as holding up the other to their poetical feeling and their human affections" (p. 201. See also H. W. Garrod, "Vergil," in *English Literature and the Classics*, ed. G. S. Gordon [Oxford, 1912]).

46. "Memorial Verses," ll. 71–74 (*Poems*, p. 164).

47. *Letters of M. A. to A. H. C.*, p. 124.

48. *Poems*, p. 2.

49. Tinker and Lowry, *op. cit.*, p. 291. The passage quoted occurs in "the prose outline and summary of the poem Arnold wanted to create." The outline and summary is of the greatest possible service in the interpretation of the poem.

50. *Empedocles on Etna*, Act II, ll. 242–43 (*Poems*, p. 130). Professor Douglas Bush calls these lines "the most Wordsworthian . . . . in all Arnold" (*Mythology and the Romantic Tradition in English Poetry* [Cambridge, Mass., 1937], p. 254). The discrimination is admirable; perhaps one might set beside these lines the eleventh and twelfth in "Quiet Work" (*Poems*, p. 36—there called by its simple original title "Sonnet"):

> "Still do thy sleepless ministers move on,
> Their glorious tasks in silence perfecting."

Bush's treatment of *Empedocles on Etna* is full of suggestion from the point of view here adopted.

51. *Poems*, p. 122, ll. 328–30. See Trilling, *op. cit.*, pp. 112–13.

52. See Bush, *op. cit.*, pp. 253–55.

53. The phrase "thought's slaves" occurs in a speech of Empedocles (*Poems*, p. 120, l. 249). The analogy between the slavery to thought and the slavery to passion is expressed in "Tristram and Iseult":

> "This, or some tyrannous single thought, some fit

Of passion, which subdues our souls to it,
Till for its sake alone we live and move"
                              ibid., p. 159, Part III, ll. 127–29

It is noteworthy that the two poems belong to the same collection, that of 1852.

54. Tinker and Lowry, *op. cit.*, p. 287.

55. Compare, e.g., Clough's "The Music of the World and the Soul" or "Wen Gott Betrügt Ist Wohl Betrogen" with the long chant of Empedocles in Act I, scene 2.

56. The first note to the *New Poems* (to which there is no preface) runs: "I cannot deny myself the pleasure of saying that I reprint (I cannot say *republish*, for it was withdrawn from circulation before fifty copies were sold) this poem at the request of a man of genius, whom it had the honour and the good fortune to interest,—Mr. Robert Browning" (p. 243). Both the act and the way of performing it were pleasing to Browning, as appears from his letters to Isa Blagden of July and August, 1867 (*Letters of Robert Browning*, ed. T. L. Hood [London, 1933], pp. 117–19).

57. One of the songs of Callicles, that which begins "Far, far from here" (Act I, scene 2, ll. 427–60), appeared in the *Poems* of 1853 as a distinct work entitled "Cadmus and Harmonia"; the other lyrics were reprinted in the *Poems* of 1855.

58. With these lines the drama ends.

59. "The Scholar Gipsy," ll. 181–90. The identification of "our wisest" as Goethe was made by Arnold during his American tour (Chilson Leonard, *Modern Language Notes*, XLVI [February, 1931], 119). It has been questioned with persuasive arguments by Tinker and Lowry (*op. cit.*, pp. 209–11), who find an identification as Tennyson more plausible. Arnold would never have said that Tennyson was "our wisest"; at no time in his career did he concede wisdom, even imperfect wisdom, to Tennyson. The same objection applies with almost equal force to an identification of the "one" as Carlyle.

60. Some of these interpretations I have given at greater length in "The Scholar Gipsy: An Interpretation" in *Revue anglo-américaine*, XII (February, 1935), 221.

61. The passages quoted are ll. 76–78, 79, 168. The original form of the last line was stronger: "They awe us, but they are not ours" (*Poems*, pp. 272–74).

62. *Ibid.*, p. 284.

63. *Letters*, ed. Russell, I, 62–63; see also the remarks of his daughter Eleanor in 1891, as reported in W. P. Fishback, *Recollections of Lord Coleridge* (Indianapolis, 1893), pp. 32–33.

64. *Poems*, p. 300.

65. These moving lines come early in the first scene, ll. 151–62 (*Poems*, p. 319). All that Polyphontes says in this first interchange has the most solemn dignity and the purest integrity. He is speaking a generation after the commission of his crime.

66. The context renders the general reflection even more interesting and weighty:

"I know, I know how hard it is to think
That right, that conscience pointed to a deed,
Where interest seems to have enjoin'd it too.
Most men are led by interest; and the few
Who are not, expiate the general sin,
Involv'd in one suspicion with the base.
Dizzy the path and perilous the way
Which in a deed like mine a just man treads,
But it is sometimes trodden, oh! believe it."

ll. 362–70

67. *Poems*, p. 363, l. 1508.

68. *Unpublished Letters*, pp. 40, 41. Whitridge dates the letter in which the former statement occurs merely "January," the letter in which the other occurs is fully dated, "January 11." This was to his brother-in-law, W. E. Forster, the former to Forster's wife, "K." Since it carries New Year's greeting, I should suppose it to have been written before the letter to Forster (which does not), probably within the opening week of the year.

CHAPTER III

1. C. B. Tinker and H. F. Lowry (*The Poetry of Matthew Arnold: A Commentary* [London, 1940], pp. 340–47) have printed fragments of the intended play on Lucretius and jottings concerning it in Arnold's notebooks and papers and have supplied as full an account of his interest in the theme and as suggestive an interpretation of the intended poem as we are ever likely to have. All the facts in this paragraph, except as otherwise noted, come from their account.

2. A. Haultain (ed.), *A Selection from Goldwin Smith's Correspondence* (New York, 1913), p. 182. The letter is dated January 13, 1886. The original is in the Cornell University Library. I might mention that one word in it was misread and gives a curious effect "Arthur Stanley was always interested, dear soul, in this project. I can hear him now saying to someone 'You hear he is going to bring in Caesar and Cicero' " (*for* hear *read* know).

3. This lecture remained unprinted until it appeared in *Macmillan's Magazine* in February, 1869. Arnold did not include it in any of his collections. It is one of the so-called "Third Series" of *Essays in Criticism*, collected by E. J. O'Brien; but since this work is not only out of print but exceedingly rare, references are given to its subsequent appearance in *Essays by Matthew Arnold* (Oxford, 1914). In using it as evidence of his attitudes in 1857, one must reckon with the possible danger to one's argument in the opportunity Arnold had to reshape the material in the light of his later opinions. In a prefatory note Arnold implies that he did not so reshape it: "Not only is this mode of treatment less to my taste now than it was eleven years ago, but the style, too, which is that of the doctor rather than the explorer, is a style which I have long since learnt to abandon" (*Essays* [Oxford, 1914],

p. 454). This is reassuring, although it does not quite exclude the possibility that details were changed. In general, when Arnold revised his essays, he did not add much new material: he excised what no longer contented him and introduced slight modifications in his judgments. He may originally have expressed himself in a slightly different fashion concerning the writers of the three ages he studies—the Periclean, the Augustan, and the Elizabethan—and concerning the ages themselves; it is unlikely that he changed his expression of opinions to the point that would endanger the argument I am proposing. This lecture was the first, Arnold tells us in the prefatory note, of his opening series as professor of poetry. That series occupied much more of his time in the chair than has ever been appreciated. It is not going too far to say that it was the central series of his Oxford lectures, from which every other discourse or series of discourses was a digression. I append a schedule, doubtless still incomplete, of the Oxford lectures:

1857–58. November 14. "On the Modern Element in Literature." The notice in the *Times*, November 5, under "University Intelligence" is as follows: "The Professor of Poetry (Mr. M. Arnold) will deliver (in the English language) an inaugural lecture at the Clarendon, on Saturday, the 14th of November, at 2 o'clock." At the time of his election Arnold wrote to his brother Thomas of his intention to ask that the custom of lecturing in Latin might be abrogated (Mrs. Humphry Ward, *A Writer's Recollections* [New York, 1918], I, 74–75).
May 29, 1858. A continuation of the inaugural series. There is a notice in the *Times* for May 20.
1858–59. December 4. A continuation of the inaugural series (*Times*, November 30). In January, 1859, Arnold was commissioned to inquire into "the systems of elementary education" in France and the French-speaking countries (*Letters of Matthew Arnold*, ed. G. W. E. Russell [New York, 1895], I, 77). He hoped to deliver a lecture in the second term, taking for his subject the Troubadours, but was "doubtful whether I can put it together in time" (*ibid.*, p. 79). He began his inquiries in France by March 15 (*Popular Education in France* [London, 1861], p. 1) and was prevented from lecturing in the third term by continued absence from England on his mission.
1859–60. May 14, 1860. A continuation of the inaugural series (*Times*, May 14, 1860). The wording of the notice is suggestive: "The Professor of Poetry (Mr. Arnold) will resume his introductory course of lectures upon the Modern Element in Literature. . . . ." The word "resume" suggests that he had either failed to lecture in the preceding term or had lectured on another topic. In the first term of this academic year he was so hard pressed drafting his report on his foreign mission that he was obliged to omit his lecture (*Letters*, ed. Russell, I, 110, 113–14).
1860–61. November 3. *On Translating Homer*, I (*Times*, October 25). December 8. *On Translating Homer*, II (*ibid.*, November 28). January 26, 1861. *On Translating Homer*, III (*ibid.*, January 23).

June 8. Resumption of the inaugural series, with, as special topic, "The Claim of the Celtic Race and the Claim of the Christian Religion To Have Originated Chivalrous Sentiment" (*ibid.*, May 29).

1861–62. November 30, 1861. *On Translating Homer* (*Times*, November 25; *Letters*, ed. Russell, I, 130).

March 29, 1862. Resumption of the inaugural series with, for special topic, "The Modern Element in Dante" (*Times*, March 24). It is very possible that a part of this lecture survives in "Dante and Beatrice," which Arnold gave to *Fraser's Magazine*, where it appeared in May, 1863, and which is available in the *Oxford Essays*, pp. 445–53. See *Letters*, ed. Russell, I, 185: "I have to get ready an old lecture, which I am going to give to Froude for *Fraser.*"

1862–63. November 15, 1862. "A Modern French Poet" (*Times*, November 10). The poet was almost certainly Maurice de Guérin, the essay on whom was "already in Froude's hands" by November 19 (*Letters*, ed. Russell, I, 176); it appeared in *Fraser's* for January, 1863.

March 26, 1863. Resumption of the inaugural series with, for special topic, "The Modern Element in Romanticism" (*Times*, March 19).

June 13, 1863. "Heinrich Heine" (*ibid.*, June 9; *Letters*, ed. Russell, I, 193).

1863–64. November 28, 1863. "A French Coleridge" (*Times*, November 26; *Letters*, ed. Russell, I, 205). When first published, in the *National Review*, for January, 1864, the essay was entitled "Joubert; or a French Coleridge." With its appearance in the first edition of *Essays in Criticism* the title was again changed, this time to "Joubert," and it has continued to bear this last of the three titles.

March 5, 1864. "Pagan and Christian Religious Sentiment" (*Times*, March 5; *Letters*, ed. Russell, I, 229). Arnold explains that, although the lecture is to appear in the *Cornhill Magazine* for April, 1864, "a good deal about Protestantism" will be left out (*Letters*, ed. Russell, I, 229); nevertheless the change of title which corresponds to the restriction in scope did not occur until the paper was collected in the *Essays in Criticism* of 1865, when it was named "Pagan and Mediaeval Religious Sentiment." The final section was never reshaped to fit the new conception.

June 4, 1864. "The Influence of Academies on National Spirit and Literature" (*Times*, May 31). The title was altered, when the paper was printed in the *Cornhill Magazine* for August, 1864, to that by which it has since been known, "The Literary Influence of Academies."

1864–65. October 29, 1864. "The Functions of Criticism at the Present Time" (*Times*, October 26). "Functions" was reduced to the singular when the paper was collected in the *Essays in Criticism* of 1865, after its first appearance in the *National Review* for November, 1864. Arnold had intended to lecture in the second term (*Letters*, ed. Russell, I, 248); but the *Times* carried an announcement on March 23, 1865, that "the lecture of the Professor of Poetry is put off till next Term." In that term also he was unable to deliver a lecture: he had been appointed by the

Schools Inquiry Commission to examine secondary education on the Continent and was absent throughout the term (*Letters*, ed. Russell, I, 244–89; *Schools and Universities on the Continent* [London, 1868], p. v).

1865–66. December 6, 1865. "The Study of Celtic Literature, I" (*Times*, November 24, where there is an announcement of this and the following lecture).

December 7, 1865. "The Study of Celtic Literature, II."

February 24, 1866. "The Study of Celtic Literature, III" (*ibid.*, February 19).

May 26, 1866. "The Study of Celtic Literature, IV" (*ibid.*, May 18). It is worth remark that the announcement sets this lecture off from the preceding, with the title "The Celtic Element in English Poetry."

1866–67. June 1, 1867. "Culture and Its Enemies" (*Times*, May 28; *Letters*, ed. Russell, I, 364). The preparation of his report on his [Continental mission of 1865 pressed heavily upon his time and energy in 1866 and 1867 (*Letters*, ed. Russell, I, 334–49), and he was not free of it until March. He could lecture only in the third term.

4. "Obermann Once More," ll. 97–104 (*The Poems of Matthew Arnold, 1840–1867*, ed. Sir. Arthur Quiller-Couch [London, 1942] [cited hereafter as "*Poems*"], p. 436).

5. See n. 3 and especially the reference to the paper on Dante and Beatrice.

6. "To a Friend," *Poems*, p. 40.

7. *Letters of Matthew Arnold to Arthur Hugh Clough*, ed. H. F. Lowry (London, 1932), p. 143.

8. "Homer himself is eternally interesting; he is a greater poetical power than even Sophocles or Aeschylus; but his age is less interesting than himself" (*Oxford Essays*, p. 467).

9. *Ibid.*, p. 246.

10. *Ibid.*, p. 268.

11. *Ibid.*, p. 401.

12. *Ibid.*, p. 312.

13. *Ibid.*, p. 385.

14. "The Two Boyhoods" in *Modern Painters*, Part IX, chap. ix. In sight of the end of his gigantic enterprise, Ruskin grapples with the problem presented by his insistence on the primary value of ideas in painting in a work advocating the greatness of a painter who was in fact weak in ideas. The solution is a mixture of rhetoric and dogma.

15. "Homeric Translation in Theory and Practice: A Reply to Matthew Arnold Esq., Professor of Poetry, Oxford," reprinted along with Arnold's Homeric lectures in the *Oxford Essays*.

16. *Oxford Essays*, p. 316.

17. *Ibid.*, p. 317.

18. *Ibid.*, pp. 421–22.

19. Arnold's reference to *David Copperfield* is in the second part of "The Incompatibles" which first appeared in the *Nineteenth Century* for June,

1881, and was later collected in *Irish Essays and Others* (London, 1882). He would have the reader believe that he had read the book earlier: "Mr. Gladstone solaced himself with it after his illness, and so set all good Liberals (of whom I wish to be considered one) upon reading it over again" (*Irish Essays*, p. 61). He says, however, in a letter to his colleague in the Education Department, J. G. Fitch, written in the preceding autumn, that he is "reading *David Copperfield* for the first time" (*Letters*, ed. Russell, II, 184). Arnold's unwillingness to make public admission that he was thirty years late in reading the novel is significant.

20. *Oxford Essays*, p. 384; T. S. Omond, "Arnold and Homer," in *Essays and Studies by Members of the English Association* (Oxford, 1912), III, 71.

21. Ichabod C. Wright, *A Letter to the Dean of Canterbury, on the Homeric Lectures of Matthew Arnold* (London, 1864).

22. *Oxford Essays*, p. 251.

23. *Ibid.*, p. 284.

24. The most revelatory of his early remarks on his work in the Education Department are those to Clough, December, 1851 (*Letters of M. A. to A. H. C.*, p. 118), and to his wife, October, 1851 (*Letters*, ed. Russell, I, 17).

25. These documents were collected by his colleague in the Education Department, Sir Francis (later Lord) Sandford, in 1889 as *Reports on Elementary Schools 1852–1882* (London, 1889). Up to 1872 he reported annually, unless prevented by his work on the reports of his foreign missions; after that year, biennially.

26. *Popular Education in France* (London, 1861), pp. xxxviii–xxxix. It is instructive to note how certain phrases were modified when the preface was reprinted in *Mixed Essays* (1879) under the title "Democracy," where the corresponding passage reads: "In all the remarks which I have been making, I have hitherto abstained from any attempt to suggest a positive application of them. I have limited myself to simply pointing out in how changed a world of ideas we are living; I have not sought to go further and to discuss in what particular manner the world of facts is to adapt itself to this changed world of ideas. This has been my rule so far; but from this rule I shall here venture to depart, in order to dwell for a moment on a matter of practical institution, designed to meet new social exigencies: on the intervention of the State in public education" (*Mixed Essays* [1st ed.; London, 1879], p. 33). The revised phrasing is much less emphatic in humility: the dropping of "impose" in the first sentence, of "presume," in the second; the total recasting of the remainder of the passage, getting rid of the "Without offensiveness" and the very Heepish "an isolated individual, however humble." The doubt whether more than diagnosis should be attempted at that time, by anyone, in any way, is also excised. Other changes, if less striking, play a part in altering the general tone of the passage. It is clear that the attitude toward the disinterested ideal has undergone a sweeping change.

27. Until the Education Act of 1870 came into force, Church of England

schools were inspected by clergy of that church, Roman Catholic schools by members of that denomination. Arnold's function was confined to the inspection of "schools connected with the British and Foreign School Society, Wesleyan, and other Protestant schools not connected with the Church of England" ([Sir Joshua] J. G. Fitch, *Thomas and Matthew Arnold and Their Influence on English Education* [New York, 1897], p. 176).

28. "The Twice-Revised Code," *Fraser's Magazine*, LXV (March, 1862), 357–58.

29. *Ibid.*, pp. 364, 359.

30. The paper on Eugénie de Guérin appeared in the *Cornhill Magazine* for June, 1863, and was composed in May (*Letters*, ed. Russell, I, 186–91). It was collected in the first series of *Essays in Criticism*.

31. The essay on Marcus Aurelius appeared in the *Victoria Magazine* for November, 1863, and was also collected in the first series of *Essays in Criticism*.

32. The articles all appeared in *Macmillan's Magazine* during 1863, "The Bishop and the Philosopher" in January, "Dr. Stanley's Lectures on the Jewish Church" in February, and "A Word More about Spinoza" in December. The last-named was originally intended for the *Times*, as appears in *Letters*, ed. Russell I, 183, 190, 208. The text of the paper on Stanley is conveniently accessible in the *Oxford Essays*, that of the paper on Spinoza in the "Everyman" collection of Arnold's periodical text of all the essays which appeared in the first series of *Essays in Criticism*.

33. *Macmillan's Magazine*, VII (January, 1863), 241.

34. *Ibid.*, p. 242.

35. *Ibid.*, p. 241.

36. *Ibid.*, p. 245.

37. *Ibid.*, pp. 245–46.

38. *Ibid.*, p. 246.

39. *Letters*, ed. Russell, I, 180, 182, 183, 188–89.

40. Clough's article had appeared in 1854 (see chap. i, n. 5); Coleridge's article (which, unlike Clough's, momentarily strained a friendship) appeared in the *Christian Remembrancer*, XXVII (April, 1854), 310–33. Arnold's feelings are described in E. H. Coleridge, *The Life and Correspondence of John Duke Coleridge, Lord Chief Justice of England* (London, 1904), I, 208–12; and by Lord Coleridge himself in *New Review*, I (July, 1889), 122.

41. *Oxford Essays*, p. 444.

42. *Ibid.*, p. 437.

43. *Ibid.*

44. "Spinoza and Professor Arnold," *Spectator*, January 3, 1863.

45. *Oxford Essays*, p. 427.

46. *Ibid.*, p. 436.

47. *Essays in Criticism* [First Series] (1st ed.: London, 1865), p. 27.

48. *Oxford Essays*, p. 436.

49. *Letters*, ed. Russell, I, 180.

50. *Ibid.*, p. 194.

51. *Ibid.*, p. 201.

52. The extraordinary pleasantness and charm of *A French Eton* has been noted by many of Arnold's interpreters, e.g., George Saintsbury, *Matthew Arnold* (New York, 1899), pp. 79–83, an appreciation which culminates in the judgment: "He never wrote better." The tone is suggested, and the need for this particular tone, in a letter Arnold wrote to Francis Palgrave in December, 1863, when he was at work on the *French Eton* papers. He praises a recent article of Palgrave's because "it has a moderation which, to say the truth, I have not always noticed in you, and it is because of the pleasure it gives me to see this, that I write these lines. True doctrine you have always had, but in trying to heal the British demoniac this is not enough; one must convey the true doctrine with studied moderation, for if one commits the least extravagance the poor madman seizes hold of this, tears and rends it, and quite fails to perceive that you have said anything else" (G. F. Palgrave, *Francis Turner Palgrave: His Journals and Memories of His Life* [London, 1899], pp. 84–85).

53. *A French Eton or Middle-Class Education and the State* (1st ed.; London, 1864), p. 66.

CHAPTER IV

1. *Letters of Matthew Arnold*, ed. G. W. E. Russell (New York, 1895), I, 247.

2. The frequency with which Goethe's name, and rather more than his name, recurs is an aspect of the method in these *Essays* which has not received sufficient notice. His praise of Schiller for rising, and aiding others in rising, above the commonplace is the theme of the closing sentences of the Preface; he is brought in to show Wordsworth's inadequacy on the side of criticism in the opening pages of "The Function of Criticism"; the superiority of his achievement to that of the English Romantics is also touched on in that essay; he is among the authors that Maurice de Guérin read; Heine is his continuator; Joubert has an ethical "sentence worthy of Goethe"; his admiration for Spinoza is commented upon at length.

3. *Essays in Criticism* [First Series] (1st ed.; London, 1865), p. 84.

4. *Ibid.*, p. 109.

5. *Ibid.*, p. 86.

6. *Ibid.*, p. 218.

7. *Ibid.*, p. 232.

8. *Ibid.*, p. 241.

9. *Ibid.*, pp. 248–52.

10. The phrase recurs in Part I, ll. 22, 126; Part III, l. 64 (*The Poems of Matthew Arnold, 1840–1867*, ed. Sir Arthur Quiller-Couch [London, 1942] [cited hereafter as "*Poems*"], pp. 238, 241, 256).

11. Part III, ll. 211–12.

12. "Thyrsis," ll. 201–2, 159, 238 (*Poems*, pp. 390–92). The contrast between light and darkness is an essential part of the structure of "Thyrsis," the falling of darkness as the poet at last descries the signal elm being a

symbol of his currently inadequate devotion to the ideal which is at last to be replenished.

13. Part III, ll. 509–19 (*Poems*, p. 267). Note Joubert's observation "Let your cry be for free souls rather even than for free men" (*Essays in Criticism* [First Series], p. 247). Arnold exaggerates Joubert's aversion from the political.

14. *Essays in Criticism* [First Series], p. 292.

15. *Ibid.*, p. 65.

16. *Letters*, ed. Russell, I, 111–12.

17. *Essays in Criticism* [First Series], pp. xviii–xix.

18. *Ibid.*, pp. 38–39.

19. *Ibid.*, p. 35.

20. *Ibid.*, pp. 189–90.

21. *Ibid.*, pp. 137–39. The approach to Lacordaire and his school at Sorèze in *A French Eton* is no less respectful and more fervent; for Arnold, Lacordaire is at once a highly poetic figure, marked by "serenity" and "sincerity" as well as by unction, and a born leader, a moral force of the first order. The combination of the poetic and the moral as they were not combined in England was what drew him now, and so often in the sequel, to the great personages of the Roman Catholic church and to the movements they led.

22. *Essays in Criticism* [First Series], p. 12.

23. *Ibid.*, p. 53.

24. *Ibid.*, pp. 84–85.

25. *Ibid.*, pp. 168–69.

26. *Ibid.*, p. 228.

27. *Ibid.*, p. 56. In the second edition (London, 1869) Arnold celebrates in a footnote the abandonment of the eccentric spelling by the *Times* (p. 53).

28. *Ibid.*, p. 231.

29. *Ibid.*, p. 111.

30. *Ibid.*, p. 174. "The magic of Heine's poetical form is incomparable." Arnold's one example in the original German is far from impressive:

> "Siehst sehr sterbeblässlich aus,
> Doch getrost! du bist zu Haus."

Of the fifteenth idyl of Theocritus he remarks "how excellent is that form, how masterly!" (*ibid.*, p. 198).

31. Irving Babbitt, *The Masters of Modern French Criticism* (Boston, 1912), p. 35. Babbitt's regard for Arnold's judgment leads him to make his chapter on Joubert a supplement to Arnold's essay.

32. *Matthew Arnold's Note Books, with a Preface by the Hon. Mrs. Wodehouse* (London, 1902), p. 2 (1857); p. 9 (1859), the first entry for the year; p. 17 (1863), again the first entry; p. 23 (1868), the second entry for the year; p. 107 (1883).

33. *Essays in Criticism* [First Series], p. 208.

34. *Ibid.*, p. 192. In the second edition (1869) by the addition of a single

word he gives to the profession of a modest intention a very different form, writing "But these great questions are not *now* for me" (p. 188).

35. Pindar and Molière are less often mentioned but when spoken of are always given eminent praise. Pindar is among his great authors in the list of 1851 (*Letters*, ed. Russell, I, 15); his poetry is linked with the dramas of Sophocles as an adequate presentation of life in "On the Modern Element in Literature" (*Oxford Essays* [Oxford, 1914], p. 464); he is set with Homer and Sophocles as a master of the grand style in the Homer lectures (*Oxford Essays*, p. 290); as a testimony to the intimacy with which Arnold entered into the spirit and art of Pindar, Gilbert Norwood's treatment of "Westminster Abbey" is notable: "Only one modern poem known to me exhibits the genuine Pindaric technique—Matthew Arnold's 'Westminster Abbey.' . . . . The spiritual light . . . . becomes a symbol dictating the language and —here comes the most finely Pindaric quality—the choice of myths" (*Pindar* [Berkeley and Los Angeles, 1945], p. 159). An expression of Arnold's admiration for Molière comes in the essay on Wordsworth where he says that Wordsworth is greater than any Continental poet since Molière except for Goethe (*Essays in Criticism, Second Series* [1st ed.; London, 1888], p. 133); the fullest treatment of his genius is in "The French Play in London," where he is spoken of as "by far the chief name in French poetry" and "one of the very greatest names in all literature," a writer with "a masterly criticism of life" gifted with a "profound seriousness" (*Irish Essays and Others* [1st ed.; London, 1882], pp. 220–21).

36. Aristotle is a more frequent object of reference than Plato; Arnold respects him profoundly both as an aesthetic and as a moral and social thinker. The references to Aristotle as an aesthetic thinker begin with Arnold's first published prose, the Preface to the *Poems* of 1853; a very large part of the poetic theory there advanced is Aristotelian and put forward explicitly as deriving from Aristotle. Aristotle is cited with equal respect in the Preface to *Merope*. "Aristotle's profound observation that the superiority of poetry over history consists in its possessing a higher truth and a higher seriousness" (*Essays in Criticism, Second Series*, p. 21) is a favorite of Arnold's in his later period of literary criticism. Arnold's use of one of Aristotle's main ethical concepts in *Culture and Anarchy* is considered in chap. v. Lord Coleridge attests that Arnold's dependence on Aristotle was even more noticeable in his conversation than in his writings (*New Review*, I [July, 1889], 114). In the last decade of his life Arnold was drawn much more powerfully to Plato than before; the *Discourses in America* abound in references to him. The supremely civilized quality of Cicero is brought out in "On the Modern Element in Literature" (*Oxford Essays*, p. 467); he exemplifies the highest in Latin literature as Shakespeare the highest in English in *Literature and Dogma* [1st ed.; London, 1873], p. xxvi); he is the only Latin writer in another list of excellence in prose given in the essay on Emerson (*Discourses in America* [1st ed.; London, 1885], p. 159). Bossuet is chosen for the perfect prose style in "The Literary Influence of Academies" (*Essays in Criticism* [First Series] [1st ed.], p. 61); and his testimony

to the true character of Jesus is cited with deep respect (*Literature and Dogma* [popular ed.; London, 1883], p. 139, n. 2). Arnold's knowledge of Burke goes back to his childhood, when Lord Coleridge recalls him "a little fellow full of cleverness, and I do not say forced, but certainly unusually forward. To say, by heart, for example, whole pages of Burke's speech on the Nabob of Arcot's debts, and to say them with real intelligence and appreciation, was certainly out of the common way in a boy of no more than seven or eight years old" (*New Review*, I [July, 1889], 112). Burke is called "our greatest English prose-writer" in "The Literary Influence of Academies" (*Essays in Criticism* [First Series], p. 61); he is, from the time of "The Function of Criticism" to the end of Arnold's life, his main British guide in matters of political thought, and in the papers on Ireland he is used as a forerunner; in one of the last of Arnold's political articles, "The Zenith of Conservatism" (*Nineteenth Century*, January, 1887), Burke's opinions are treated as canonical. Arnold's regard for the author of the *Imitation of Christ* and for Goethe is too well known to require any illustration.

37. *Essays in Criticism* [First Series], 1st ed., p. 214.

38. *Ibid.*, p. 215.

39. *Ibid.*, p. 38.

40. *Ibid.*, p. 274.

41. *Ibid.*, p. 186. A very different judgment on Byron's intellect is given in the essay on Byron in the second series of *Essays in Criticism*.

42. *Essays in Criticism* [First Series], 1st ed., p. 206.

43. *Letters*, ed. Russell, I, 127-28.

44. See chap. iii, n. 3.

45. *Essays in Criticism* [First Series], 1st ed., p. 223.

46. *Letters*, ed. Russell, I, 158, "I had rather live in a purer air than that of controversy, and when I have done two more things I must do,—an article on Middle-Class Education [this developed into *A French Eton*] and one on Academies (such as the French Academy) both of which will raise opposition and contradiction,—I mean to leave this region altogether and to devote myself wholly to what is positive and happy, not negative and contentious, in literature."

47. *Essays in Criticism* [First Series], 1st ed., p. 61. No argument of any kind is offered to sustain this opinion.

48. In his Preface to *Six Selected Lives from Johnson's Lives of the English Poets* (London, 1878), he argues that an adequate English prose was the most notable achievement of the literature of the eighteenth century. Dryden, Addison, and Swift receive his highest praise as examples of the new prose style.

49. *Essays in Criticism* [First Series], 1st ed., p. x.

50. *Ibid.*, pp. 28-29.

51. *Ibid.*, p. 74.

52. *Ibid.*, pp. 188-89.

53. *On the Study of Celtic Literature* (1st ed.; London, 1867), pp. 179-81.

54. *Irish Essays and Others* (1st ed.; London, 1882), p. 16. Burke's sentence occurs in his *A Letter to Sir Hercules Langrishe, Bart. M.P. on the Subject of the Roman Catholics of Ireland* (*Works* ["Bohn Classics"], III, 321).

55. *On the Study of Celtic Literature*, 1st ed., p. 181.

56. *Ibid.*, pp. 180–81.

57. *Ibid.*, pp. 31–32.

58. *Ibid.*, p. 73.

59. *Ibid.*, p. 181.

60. *Ibid.*, p. 10.

61. *Ibid.*, p. 86.

62. *Ibid.*, pp. 85–86.

63. *Ibid.*, p. 120.

64. *Ibid.*, pp. 17–18.

65. *Letters*, ed. Russell, I, 320. The rest of the passage is also very downright: "Jane [his sister], too, to whom I spoke of this, is clearly of the same opinion, and indeed I have not a doubt of it. He thought our rule in Ireland cruel and unjust, no doubt. He was not blind to faults in the Saxon; but can you show me a single line, in all he has written, testifying to his sense of any virtues and graces in the Celt?" Thomas Arnold's doctrine concerning Ireland was in essence that the Irish were a nation and entitled to be masters in their own house; that the Roman Catholic church was a part of Christendom; and that the prospect of an Ireland dominated in religion by this church ought not to be frustrated by what religious preferences the English might have (see his letters to Whately, archbishop of Dublin, November 8, 1833; to W. Empson, June 11, 1834; and again to Whately, May 16, 1836, in A. P. Stanley, *Life of Thomas Arnold* [1st American ed.; New York, 1845]).

66. *On the Study of Celtic Literature*, 1st ed., p. 18.

67. *Ibid.*, p. 72.

68. *Ibid.*, p. 47.

69. *Ibid.*, p. 50.

70. *Ibid.*, pp. 101–2, 109–10.

71. *Ibid.*, p. 135.

72. *Ibid.*, p. 170.

73. *Ibid.*, pp. 115–16.

74. *Ibid.*, p. 181. In the original text Arnold made the plea for a chair of Celtic at much greater length (*Cornhill Magazine*, XIV [July, 1866], 127–28). I have reproduced it in *Studies in the Text of Matthew Arnold's Prose Works* (Paris, 1935), pp. 14–16, and in *Representative Essays of Matthew Arnold* (Toronto, 1936), Appen., pp. 237–39. That the foundation of a chair of Celtic at Oxford was among the purposes of the lectures is made plain in *Letters*, ed. Russell, I, 332.

CHAPTER V

1. *Letters of Matthew Arnold*, ed. G. W. E. Russell (New York, 1895), I, 250–51. His sense of education as a phase of society appears in the expression "I have here an opportunity of seeing at comparative leisure, and with

all possible facilities given me, some of the most important concerns of the most powerful and interesting States of the Continent."

2. *Ibid.* It was understood that he should compose his report after he had resumed his ordinary duties as inspector.

3. *Schools and Universities on the Continent* (1st ed.; London, 1868), pp. 271–72.

4. *Ibid.*, p. 273.

5. *Letters*, ed. Russell, I, 335.

6. "I remember my father, in one of his unpublished letters written more than forty years ago, when the political and social state of the country was gloomy and troubled, and there were riots in many places, goes on, after strongly insisting on the badness and foolishness of the government, and on the harm and dangerousness of our feudal and aristocratical constitution of society, and ends thus: 'As for rioting, the old Roman way of dealing with *that* is always the right one; flog the rank and file, and fling the ring-leaders from the Tarpeian Rock.' And this opinion we can never forsake" (*Culture and Anarchy*, ed. J. Dover Wilson [Cambridge, 1932], p. 203). The passage was excised from the second edition, that of 1875. It has been severely criticized by J. M. Robertson in *Modern Humanists* (London, 1891), pp. 166–67. It is fair to set beside this passage, in which Matthew Arnold supports his father's well-known zeal for the rod, another, almost contemporary, passage in which he remarks "of flogging . . . . one may say the modern spirit has irrevocably condemned it as a school punishment, so that it will more and more come to appear half-disgusting, half-ridiculous, and a teacher will find it more and more difficult to inflict it without a loss of self-respect" (*Schools and Universities on the Continent*, pp. 80–81).

7. *Letters*, ed. Russell, I, 377. "I was dining at the Garrick Club last night, when one of the guests came in saying that his hansom had been nearly knocked down by a string of cabs with policemen filling them inside and out, hurrying to Clerkenwell Prison, which had been blown up by the Fenians. . . . . You know I have never wavered in saying that the Hyde Park business eighteen months ago was fatal, and that a Government which dared not deal with a mob, of any nation or with any design, simply opened the floodgates to anarchy" (see also, *ibid.*, pp. 379–80).

8. "The Philistines, who among their other sins are the guilty authors of Fenianism." The phrase comes in the closing sentence of the book *On the Study of Celtic Literature* ([1st ed.; London, 1867], p. 181).

9. See n. 7, *supra*.

10. *Letters*, ed. Russell, I, 377.

11. *Ibid.*, p. 382.

12. "My Countrymen," *Cornhill Magazine*, XIII (February, 1866). The text of the periodical article was reprinted as an appendix to the edition of *The Study of Celtic Literature* in the "Everyman Library." For convenience, references to the text will be made to this edition. Fitzjames Stephen had assailed the essay on "The Functions of Criticism at the Present Time"

in the *Saturday Review*, XVIII (December 3, 1864), 683-85, under the title "Mr. Matthew Arnold and His Countrymen."

13. *The Study of Celtic Literature* ("Everyman" ed.; London, 1932), pp. 196-97.

14. The revised version runs: "Instead of confining myself to what alone I had any business with,—the slow and obscure work of trying to understand things, to see them as they are,—I had been meddling with practice, proposing this and that, saying how it might be if we established this or that. So I was suffering deservedly in being taunted with hawking about my nostrums of State schools for a class much too wise to want them, and of an Academy for people who have an inimitable style already. To be sure, I had said that schools ought to be things of local, not State, institution and management, and that we ought not to have an Academy; but that makes no difference. I saw what danger I had been running by thus intruding into a sphere where I have no business, and I resolved to offend in this way no more" (*Friendship's Garland* [1st ed.; London, 1871], p. 120). There appears to be a real wish to minimize polemics in this revision; all the instances of what in an unpolemical manner he will refrain from saying are omitted; and the excision of the scriptural statement—"the beautiful and appropriate Scriptural quotation" as the *Saturday Review* ironically styled it (XXI [February 10, 1866] 161)—is also an unmistakable instance of pacific temper. The removal of the phrase "one of my own cardinal rules" is proper in one who had in the interim, notably in *Culture and Anarchy*, disobeyed the principle more often than he had obeyed it.

15. *On The Study of Celtic Literature*, 1st ed., pp. vi-viii.

16. See chap. ii, n. 1.

17. *Times* ("University Intelligence"), May 28, 1867; *Letters*, ed. Russell, I, 364.

18. *Cornhill Magazine*, XVI (July, 1867), 52.

19. Wilson, *op. cit.*, p. 52.

20. *Ibid.*, p. 58.

21. Arnold's original intention was to write but one article on this topic, "a sort of pendant to *Culture and its Enemies*, to be called *Anarchy and Authority*, and to appear in the Christmas *Cornhill*" (*Letters*, ed. Russell, I, 376). The single article expanded into five.

22. Wilson, *op. cit.*, p. vii.

23. *Ibid.*, p. 86.

24. *Ibid.*, pp. 89-90.

25. *Ibid.*, p. 86.

26. *Ibid.*, p. vii.

27. *Ibid.*, pp. 72-73.

28. *Ibid.*, p. 82.

29. *Ibid.*, p. 96. It is noteworthy how Arnold reiterates the claim at the end of each section in his argument.

30. *Ibid.*, p. xxxi.

31. Cf. *Letters*, ed. Russell, I, 309, where Arnold says that, failing a due

complement of ideas, England is in danger of "losing immeasurably in all ways, declining into a sort of greater Holland."

32. Wilson, *op. cit.*, p. 87.

33. *Ibid.*, p. 95.

34. *Ibid.*, pp. 205–6.

35. Frederic Harrison made the charge in "Culture: A Dialogue," *Fortnightly Review*, VIII (November, 1867), 603–14, collected in Harrison's *The Choice of Books* (London, 1886), pp. 97–119. Arnold frequently quotes the phrase in whole or in part (e.g., Wilson, *op. cit.*, p. 85).

36. The absence of the terms from the valedictory and from the papers on "Anarchy and Authority" is made more striking by the frequency with which they occur in the Preface, composed in 1869. Examples: "But now to evince the disinterestedness which culture teaches us" (Wilson, *op. cit.*, p. 23); "If culture is the disinterested endeavour after man's perfection" (p. 27); "That is because culture, disinterestedly trying in its aim at perfection" (p. 30); "But now as we have shown the disinterestedness which culture enjoins" (p. 33); "When we see that culture not only makes a quite disinterested choice of the machinery proper to carry us towards sweetness and light, and to make reason and the will of God prevail, but by even this machinery does not hold stiffly and blindly, and easily passes on beyond it to that for the sake of which it chose it" (p. 33).

37. Stuart Sherman, *Matthew Arnold: How To Know Him* (Indianapolis, 1917), pp. 228–29.

38. Wilson, *op. cit.*, p. 41.

39. *Letters*, ed. Russell, II, 34.

40. The praise of Heine as a soldier in the welfare for the liberation of humanity dominates the essay on Heine. A liberal is one who acts as a dissolvent of the *ancien régime*. The link with Arnold's own aims is explicit in this remark: "Dissolvents of the old European system of dominant ideas and facts we must all be, all of us who have any power of working; what we have to study is that we may not be acrid dissolvents of it" (*Essays in Criticism* [First Series] [1st ed.; London, 1865], p. 155).

41. W. E. Forster had married Matthew Arnold's sister "K" and had acquired at least as intimate a relation with Arnold as if he were a blood brother. Arnold's letter to him concerning *Merope* is one of the most profound he ever wrote (*Unpublished Letters of Matthew Arnold*, ed. Arnold Whitridge [New Haven, Conn., 1923], pp. 34–40).

42. His warfare against the policy of his chiefs came to its climax in his article "The Twice Revised Code" (1862). See chap. iii, p. 67. Arnold was prepared to risk dismissal for his activities (*Letters*, ed. Russell, I, 168). Harriet Martineau, an exigent critic, indorsed Lord Lansdowne's liberalism in *Biographical Sketches* (New York, 1869), pp. 329–37. The contrast between Lansdowne and his pseudo-liberal successors was galling.

43. Wilson, *op. cit.*, p. 211.

44. *Ibid.*, p. 210.

45. *Letters*, ed. Russell, I, 392.

46. *Ibid.*, p. 201 (1863).

47. Carlyle early lost all belief in parliamentary democracy. His attitude toward both English parties is well summed up in his remark to a great soldier, Lord Wolseley, toward the end of his life: "Well, Sir, I am glad to have made your acquaintance, and I wish you well. There is one duty which I hope may yet be laid upon you before you leave this world—to lock the door of yonder place [The House of Commons], and turn them all out about their business" (J. A. Froude, *Thomas Carlyle: A History of His Life in London, 1834–1881* [London, 1884], II, 447). Ruskin's mature opinion is expressed in a letter to the students at Glasgow when he was a candidate for the lord rectorship of the university in 1880: "Had you ever read ten words of mine with understanding you would have known that I care no more either for Mr. D'Israeli or Mr. Gladstone than for two old bagpipes with the drones going by steam, but that I hate all Liberalism as I do Beelzebub, and that, with Carlyle, I stand, we two alone now in England, for God and the Queen" (E. T. Cook, *Life of John Ruskin* [London, 1911], II, 441).

48. Wilson, *op. cit.*, p. 8.

49. Archdeacon Denison wrote to an inspector as follows: "I love you very much; but, if you ever come here again to inspect, I lock the door of the school, and tell the boys to put you in the pond" (G. W. E. Russell, *Collections and Recollections* [New York, 1898], p. 336). See also Frank Smith, *History of English Elementary Education, 1760–1902* (London, 1931).

50. Wilson, *op. cit.*, pp. 75–76.

51. *Ibid.*, p. 212.

52. *Ibid.*, p. 96.

CHAPTER VI

1. Neither *On Translating Homer* nor *On the Study of Celtic Literature* was reprinted in England in the lifetime of the author. The only one of the educational works to fare better was *Schools and Universities on the Continent*, of which the part concerned with Germany was reprinted in 1874 under the title *Higher Schools and Universities in Germany*.

2. *Letters of Matthew Arnold*, ed. G. W. E. Russell (New York, 1895), II, 47. The italics are Arnold's.

3. *Ibid.*, p. 92.

4. *Ibid.*, pp. 3–4. Arnold dealt in the Preface to *Culture and Anarchy* with the severe critique of his *Schools and Universities on the Continent* written for the *Quarterly* by Oscar Browning and implied, at least, a strong condemnation of William Smith for allowing the book to be appraised by a master at Eton, who could scarcely offer a disinterested judgment of the educational writings of an author who was aiming at a truly national system of secondary education and making incidental criticisms of the British public schools (*Culture and Anarchy*, ed. John Dover Wilson [Cambridge, 1932], pp. 8–10). The passage was excised after the pleasant meeting with William Smith. Arnold wrote two articles for the *Quarterly* some years afterward; up to this time he had never been among its authors.

5. *Letters*, ed. Russell, II, 6. The bishop of Derry, William Alexander, had been among the earliest admirers of Arnold's poetry and had expressed the admiration at length in his *Afternoon Lectures on Literature and Art* (4th ser., 1867). In 1867 Arnold reports that the bishop had told him that "my poems were the centre of his mental life, and that he had read many of them hundreds of times" (*Letters*, ed. Russell, II, 131).

6. *Letters*, ed. Russell, II, 23.

7. *Ibid.*, p. 35.

8. *Ibid.*, p. 51.

9. John Morley in his *Recollections* ([New York, 1917] Book I, chap. vii) devotes several pages to Arnold and regrets that Arnold should have supposed him at all deficient in gratitude for the illumination he had received from both the poetry and the critical prose.

10. *Letters*, ed. Russell, II, 125.

11. *Ibid.*, pp. 19, 82.

12. *Ibid.*, p. 43. See also his letter to his sister (*ibid.*, p. 39), where he says that as his years for effective work in his own line decrease, the thought of the "interruption caused by the continual travelling-about which inspection requires becomes trying"; and also his letter to his mother (*ibid.*, p. 69).

13. "A Persian Passion Play" was written for delivery as a lecture to the Birmingham and Midland Institute in October, 1871; it appeared in the *Cornhill* for December.

14. The essay "My Countrymen" appeared in the *Cornhill* for February, 1866; other parts appeared in the *Pall Mall Gazette* in 1866 and 1867.

15. *St. Paul and Protestantism* (1st ed.; London, 1870), p. 91.

16. *Ibid.*, p. 94.

17. *Ibid.*, p. 93.

18. *Ibid.*, p. 95.

19. *Ibid.*, p. 151.

20. *Letters*, ed. Russell, II, 44-45.

21. *St. Paul and Protestantism*, 1st. ed., pp. xvii–xix.

22. *Ibid.* (popular ed.; London, 1887), p. 131, n. 1. "Mr. Wintersbotham has since died. Nothing in my remarks on his speech need prevent me from expressing here my high esteem for his character, accomplishments, oratorical faculty and general promise, and my sincere regret for his loss."

23. See, e.g., his attack on a leading Congregationalist, Edward Miall, the editor of the *Nonconformist:* "Mialism is a sub-form of Hebraism, and itself a somewhat spurious and degenerated form; but the sub-form always tends to degenerate into forms lower yet, and yet more unworthy of the ideal flower of Hebraism" (*St. Paul and Protestantism*, 1st ed., p. xxxv).

24. *Letters*, ed. Russell, II, 36.

25. *Ibid.*, p. 135. The letter is to Henry Nettleship, later professor of Latin at Oxford. See also W. W. Jackson, *Ingram Bywater* (Oxford, 1917), p. 105. Bywater was one of the prime movers.

26. *Letters*, ed. Russell, II, 136. The letter is to G. W. Boyle, later dean

of Salisbury, a younger man who later paid very high tribute to Arnold's intellectual power in his *Recollections* (London, 1899), p. 180.

27. "Keble voted for me after all. . . . . I had support from all sides. Archdeacon Denison voted for me, also Sir John Yarde Buller, and Henley, of the High Tory party. It was an immense victory." These sentences are from a letter written by Matthew Arnold to his mother shortly after the election of May, 1857 (Mrs. Humphry Ward, *A Writer's Recollections* [New York, 1918], I, 76). Keble was Arnold's godfather (Thomas Arnold, *Passages in a Wandering Life* [London, 1900], p. 15).

28. John Campbell Shairp, *Aspects of Poetry, Being Lectures Delivered at Oxford* (Boston, 1882), p. 33. The sentence quoted is followed by another implied reservation no less interesting: "Even when we may not agree with all he says, his words instruct and delight us; for every word he speaks *on these subjects* is living, based on large knowledge, and on a high standard of excellence." The reservation is the more significant that Shairp always speaks of Arnold's purely literary criticism with the deepest respect. He had reprehended Arnold's social criticism much earlier, as showing a failure to give the first place to religion, in *Culture and Religion in Some of Their Relations* (Edinburgh, 1871), chap. iii, "The Literary Theory of Culture."

29. *Literature and Dogma* (1st ed.; London, 1873), p. 8. The earlier statement of these ideas almost in the same language occurs in "The Function of Criticism" (*Essays in Criticism* [First Series] [1st ed.; London, 1865], pp. 37-38).

30. *Literature and Dogma* is the only one of Arnold's works of which *a part* appeared in a periodical. In my *Studies in the Text of Matthew Arnold's Prose Works* (Paris, 1935) I have given reasons for believing that editor or publisher or both objected to the material and abruptly terminated arrangements for its appearance. My inferences have been challenged by William Blackburn in his article, "The Background of Arnold's *Literature and Dogma*" (*Modern Philology*, XLIII [November, 1945], 130-39). Without attempting an elaborate argument, which would be out of place here, I wish to quote the final sentence of the second instalment: "But to finish our defence of literature against dogma we need one paper more; and perhaps our remarks on miracles will come better at the beginning of that than at the end of this" (*Cornhill Magazine*, XXIV [October, 1871], 492). No third instalment appeared.

31. The publication of *A French Eton* in *Macmillan's Magazine* was interrupted because of Arnold's falling behind with his material (*Letters*, ed. Russell, I, 226); there was a similar break in the series on "Anarchy and Authority," for the same reason (*ibid.*, p. 390).

32. *Literature and Dogma*, 1st ed., pp. v-vi.

33. *Ibid.*, pp. vii-viii.

34. *Ibid.*, p. xiv.

35. *Ibid.*, esp. pp. xvi-xx.

36. *Ibid.*, p. 278.

37. *Ibid.*, p. 288.

38. *Ibid.*, p. 347.

39. The allusions at the end of chap. vii (p. 248) and chap. xi (p. 362) are especially acid.

40. Under the title "A Review of Objections to Literature and Dogma," the work which was later to be entitled *God and the Bible* began to appear in the *Contemporary Review* in October, 1874. It was of this opening paper that Sir Leslie Stephen, the editor of the *Cornhill*, remarked: "It is Mat in excelsis—the very cheekiest production I have yet seen of his" (F. W. Maitland, *Life and Letters of Leslie Stephen* [London, 1906], p. 245).

41. *God and the Bible* (1st ed.; London, 1875), pp. 22–23.

42. *Ibid.*, pp. 23–24. This and, indeed, almost all that is controversial in the introduction to *God and the Bible* was omitted when the popular edition was published in 1884.

43. For Huxley's retort—inspired also by indignation at the cheap rhetoric and fatuous reasoning of Bishop Wilberforce—in the debate on evolution at the Oxford meeting of the British Association in 1860 see Leonard Huxley, *Life and Letters of T. H. Huxley* (New York, 1901), I, 194–203.

44. *God and the Bible*, 1st ed., p. 377.

45. *Literature and Dogma*, popular ed., p. xii.

46. R. H. Hutton, *Criticisms on Contemporary Thought and Thinkers* (London, 1894), I, 218: "He cannot pick and choose and say that this is poetry, because he does not think its drift can be 'verified'; and that that, on the other hand, is prose, because he has persuaded himself that he has 'verified' it."

47. "When he comes down to the New Testament and Jesus, his genial method becomes so transparent as almost to supersede hostile criticism. He has an imaginary Jesus as he had an imaginary Israel" (J. M. Robertson, *Modern Humanists* [London, 1891], p. 158).

48. *Mixed Essays* (1st ed.; London, 1879), p. 271.

49. *Ibid.*, pp. 242, 252, 253, 273.

50. J. M. Robertson is correct in his claim that "Arnold's frequent attacks on Macaulay are visibly expressions of personal dislike rather than critical judgements," except that the word "personal" is misleading, for it was the Macaulay type of mind and temper, not Macaulay himself, that aroused Arnold's dislike. "They are malicious," Robertson continues, "and malice and criticism are of two houses" (*Modern Humanists Reconsidered* [London, 1927], p. 117). Without retracting any of his objections to Macaulay's positions, Arnold admitted in 1887 that the tone in which he had expressed them had been "a little hard on him" (Francis Galton, *Two Essays upon Matthew Arnold with Some of His Letters to the Author* [London, 1897], p. 117).

51. *Mixed Essays*, 1st ed., p. 236. The essay on Falkland first appeared in the *Nineteenth Century* for March, 1877.

52. *Mixed Essays*, 1st ed., p. 236.

53. "A Psychological Parallel" first appeared in the *Contemporary Review* for November, 1876.

54. *Last Essays on Church and Religion* (1st ed.; London, 1877), p. v.

55. *Ibid.*, p. vi.

56. *Essays in Criticism, Second Series* (1st ed.; London, 1888), pp. 6 ff. The essay on "The Study of Poetry" first appeared as the general introduction to *The English Poets* (London, 1880), edited by Arnold's nephew by marriage, Humphry Ward.

57. *Essays in Criticism, Second Series*, p. 44.

58. *Ibid.*, p. 122.

59. *Ibid.*, p. 153. When the essay was reprinted in 1879 as the Preface to *Poems of Wordsworth*, "elementary" was changed to "primary" (p. 21).

60. *Essays in Criticism, Second Series*, p. 154.

61. *Ibid.*, p. 126.

62. The Arnold house, Fox How, at Ambleside, was within walking distance of Wordsworth's Dove Cottage at Grasmere.

63. "I have myself heard him declare that, for he knew not how many years, his poetry had never brought him in enough to buy his shoe-strings." "I remember Wordsworth relating how one of the pilgrims, a clergyman, asked him if he had ever written anything besides the *Guide to the Lakes*. Yes, he answered modestly, he had written verses." "I remember hearing him say that 'Goethe's poetry was not inevitable enough' " (*Essays in Criticism, Second Series*, 1st ed., pp. 123, 124, 155).

64. *Ibid.*, p. 162.

65. His aversion from the professional admirers of Wordsworth was profound. In his reference to a meeting of the Wordsworth Society in 1883, he is extraordinarily emphatic: "The grave would have been cheerful compared to the view presented by the Westminster Chamber and the assembled Wordsworth Society when I came upon the platform. . . . . I have been quite bilious for the last day or two, and today, when I saw the Society drawn out before me, my tongue clave to the roof of my mouth, and I nearly began to retch" (*Letters*, ed. Russell, II, 211).

66. *Essays in Criticism, Second Series*, 1st ed., p. 162.

67. *Ibid.*, p. 172.

68. *Ibid.*, pp. 193–96. This view of Byron was an old one with Arnold; he had expressed it in the essay on Heine (*Essays in Criticism* [First Series] [1st ed.; London, 1865], pp. 170–71); but now he concedes to Byron far greater power in expressing his insight.

69. *Essays in Criticism, Second Series*, pp. 198–99.

70. *Poetical Works* ("Globe" ed.; London, 1893), pp. 479–85. Stanley died on July 25, 1881; the poem first appeared in the *Nineteenth Century* for January, 1882. One would not suppose from reading the poem side by side with "Thyrsis" that Arnold thought Stanley not "so impressive and deep-reaching a personage" as Clough (E. H. Coleridge, *Life and Correspondence of Lord Coleridge*, II [London, 1904], 309).

71. *Mixed Essays*, 1st ed., p. 61. The essay was first printed in the *Fortnightly* for March, 1878.

72. *Mixed Essays*, 1st ed., pp. 96–97.

73. *Ibid.*, p. 57.

74. *Ibid.*, p. 58.

75. *Ibid.*, p. 100.

76. *Ibid.*, p. 108.

77. *Ibid.*, p. 137. Arnold speaks of Tulloch with respect in "A Psychological Parallel," where he refers to his treatment of the Latitude men in his *Rational Theology and Christian Philosophy in England in the Seventeenth Century* (*Last Essays on Church and Religion*, p. 19). The references to Tulloch are more generous in the text of the book than they had been in that of the original article which appeared in the *Contemporary* for November, 1876.

78. Sir Leslie Stephen, *Studies of a Biographer* (New York, 1898–1902), II, 104.

79. *Irish Essays and Others* (1st ed.; London, 1882), p. 61. "The Incompatibles" had appeared in two parts in the *Nineteenth Century* for April and June, 1881. The division is retained in the book text.

80. *Irish Essays and Others*, p. 62.

81. George Saintsbury, *Matthew Arnold* (New York, 1899), pp. 151–52.

82. *Irish Essays and Others*, 1st ed., pp. 5, 6, 14, 34, 55.

83. *Ibid.*, p. vi.

84. Carleton Stanley, *Matthew Arnold* (Toronto, 1938), p. 147.

85. Morley, *op. cit.*, I, 129.

86. He resigned as inspector as of April 30, 1886. A remarkable series of political articles followed hard upon his resignation: "The Nadir of Liberalism," *Nineteenth Century*, May, 1886; "The Zenith of Conservatism," *ibid.*, January, 1887; "Up to Easter," *ibid.*, May, 1887; "From Easter to August," *ibid.*, September, 1887; "Disestablishment in Wales," *National Review*, March, 1888. Arnold had always claimed and been permitted what seems unusual freedom in political comment for a civil servant. His awareness of the freedom he had been permitted appears in a statement made after retirement: "Abroad probably a Minister might have known more about my performances; but then abroad I doubt whether I should ever have survived to perform them. Under the strict bureaucratic system abroad, I feel pretty sure that I should have been dismissed ten times over for the freedom with which on various occasions I have exposed myself on matters of Religion and Politics. Our Government here in England takes a large and liberal view about what it considers a man's private affairs, and so I have been able to survive as an Inspector for thirty-five years; and to the Government I at least owe this—to have been allowed to survive" (G. W. E. Russell, *Matthew Arnold* [New York, 1904], pp. 54–55). Chagrin mingles with appreciation: perhaps it was because of his use of such freedom that he was never promoted to one of the higher places in the Education Department in which he might have had a larger role in the formation of policy. But the essays on politics written after his retirement are more concerned with the more detailed moves in partisan controversy than is anything he had written before, except for the unsigned essay on "The Twice Revised Code."

87. *Civilization in the United States* (Boston, 1888), p. 73. This work has never circulated in Great Britain.

88. *Ibid.*, pp. 93–94.

89. *Ibid.*, p. 98. Arnold's son Richard had married an Australian; and it is interesting to note the variety of references to Australia in Arnold's later writings.

90. *Ibid.*, p. 105.

91. William C. Brownell, *Victorian Prose Masters* (New York, 1915), pp. 173–74. Brownell's consideration of this aspect of Arnold's strategy is notably illuminating: "He could not, I fancy, quite characterize us to his satisfaction. At least a tentativeness that is almost touching, certainly very charming, is to be felt in his most systematic efforts to do so. When he lectured here he was more than circumspect, he was cautious; yet at the same time he was very courageously conscientious in what he said to us and of us."

92. He was Goldwin Smith's guest at Toronto in 1884, and their friendship was greatly stimulated by the new contact.

93. *A Selection from Goldwin Smith's Correspondence*, ed. A. Haultain (New York, 1913), p. 182. The letter is dated January 13, 1886.

94. For the titles and times of the articles see n. 86, *supra*.

95. *Nineteenth Century*, XXI (May, 1887), 629.

96. For Arnold's symptoms and his interpretations of them see *Letters*, ed. Russell, II, 278, 280, 283, 315, 344, 346, 347, 357–58, 363, 376. The letter of January 29, 1887, to Mrs. Coates is especially striking: "For my part, since I was sixty I have regarded each year, as it ended, as something to the good beyond what I could naturally have expected. This summer in America I began to think that my time was really coming to an end, I had so much pain in my chest, the sign of a malady which had suddenly struck down in middle life, long before they came to my present age, both my father and my grandfather" (*ibid.*, p. 363).

97. *Ibid.*, pp. 312–13.

98. *A Selection from Goldwin Smith's Correspondence*, *loc. cit.* The MS is in the Cornell University Library. The word printed as "one" is not clearly legible; I should read it as "our."

99. *Nineteenth Century*, XIX (May, 1886), 648–54.

100. *Essays in Criticism, Second Series*, 1st ed., p. 209.

101. *Ibid.*, p. 222. Arnold has in mind T. Healy, one of the leading Home Rulers in the House of Commons, at the time the essay was written.

102. *Ibid.*, pp. 208, 213.

103. *Ibid.*, p. 237.

104. *New Review*, I (July, 1889), 112–13. "Readers of Dr. Arnold's letters, in Dean Stanley's Life, will readily believe that he did not cordially recognise the genius of his son, that of the humor and delightful persiflage of the son the father was not a very genial judge; that there was between them that 'imperfect sympathy' which Charles Lamb has so delicately de-

scribed, the fertile source of misunderstanding, the ground for much mistaken judgment. Stories are told, not to be repeated here, of the austere literalness with which Dr. Arnold restrained the lively sallies of his son, and showing that he could not see, and if he had seen that he would not have approved of those traits. . . . ."

105. Only eight pages in forty-eight.

106. Only the final paragraph of the essay concerns the poetry. In it Arnold confesses "of his poetry I have not space now to speak" (*Essays in Criticism, Second Series*, 1st ed., p. 251).

107. Lord Coleridge asserts the intention in the "prefatory note" to the *Essays*, p. vi; see also I. E. Sells, *Matthew Arnold and France* (Cambridge, 1935), p. 237, n. 3. I am informed by the Macmillan Company that many years earlier Arnold expressed interest in doing the volume on Shelley for the "English Men of Letters" series (in which he had declined to do the *Shakespeare*).

108. *Civilization in the United States*, pp. 187, 177, 189.

GENERAL INDEX

[Where there are several entries under one name, italics indicate extended reference.]

INDEX TO ARNOLD'S WORKS

[Where there are several entries under one name, italics indicate extended reference.]

PROSE

MATTHEW ARNOLD

VERSE

TO THE MINDS of most readers today the figure of Matthew Arnold is that of a dignified, serene Victorian gentleman. We see him as perfectly poised, always quite sure of himself, meeting every problem with complacent urbanity.

In this book Matthew Arnold is presented in quite a different light. He is shown to have been anxious, confused, uncertain of himself, often impulsive and violent—and wholly human.

He loved the grand manner and the great books; he sought the truths which he considered eternal and the forms in which such truths could be properly expressed.

But he also longed to work directly and powerfully on the opinion of his time, to strike a quick sharp blow for the urgent causes of the moment. He believed that the writer's first need was to be sure that his light was light indeed and not a new kind of dark-

(Continued on back flap)